The Starting Point of Happiness

The Starting Point of Happiness

A Practical and Intuitive Guide to
Discovering Love, Wisdom, and Faith

Ryuho Okawa

Lantern Books
A Division of Booklight Inc.

© Ryuho Okawa 2001

2001
Lantern Books
One Union Square West, Suite 201
New York, NY 10003

Translated by The Institute for Research in Human Happiness Ltd.
Original title: *Kofuku-no-Genten*.

Printed in the United States of America

Library of Congress Cataloging-in-Publication Data

Okawa, Ryuho, 1956–
    The starting point of happiness: a practical and intuitive
guide to discovering love, wisdom, and faith / Ryuho Okawa.
        p. cm.
ISBN 1-930051-18-2
1. Spiritual life. 2. Happiness. I. Title.

BL624.O412 2001
29.1.4—dc21

                                                    00-066319

Contents

Introduction ix

Chapter 1: The Starting Point of Happiness 1

1. The Start of Your Life on Earth 1
2. Discovering Your True Worth 3
3. Columbus's Egg 3
4. Refining Your Soul 4
5. Put Giving Love First 6
6. The Starting Point of Happiness 7

Chapter 2: On Love That Gives 9

1. Starting with Nothing 9
2. The Joy of Discovery 12
3. Reflecting on Yourself 14
4. Changing Your Perspective 15

5. Finding Light in the Darkness 17
6. The World Where Thought Is Everything 20
7. Discovering a New Perspective 21
8. Exploring Right Mind 24
9. The Watershed of Life 27
10. Toward Love That Does
    Not Expect Anything in Return 30
11. What Is the Starting Point of Happiness? 33

**Chapter 3: Embark on the Journey
to Bring Happiness to the Whole of Mankind 35**

1. The Discovery of a Great Love 35
2. The Advance of Light 37
3. Keep on Advancing, Never Retreat 38
4. Time to Transcend the Barrier
    between Self and Others 39
5. Seven Declarations for Happiness 41

Chapter 4: The Starting Point of Faith 43

1. An Encounter with God 43
2. Be Pure in Heart 45
3. Fighting the Desire to Assert the Ego 47
4. Feelings of Inferiority and Love 49
5. The Starting Point of Faith 51

Chapter 5: In Springtime .53

1. The Season of Endurance .53
2. The Torrent of Life Force .56
3. The Presence of Infinite Wisdom 59

Chapter 6: The Nature of Courage 61

1. What Is Courage? 61
2. Compassion and Courage 63
3. Leadership 66
4. The Ability to Make Decisions 67
5. The Importance of Courage 69

Chapter 7: Living a Positive Life 71

1. The Frontier Spirit 71
2. Invincible Thinking—Winning in Every Situation 73
3. A Positive Attitude 75
4. The Snowball Effect 78
5. Time to Take Flight into Infinity 80

Chapter 8: The Will of the Great Universe 83

1. The Galaxy and Human Beings 83
2. The Truth About the
   Three-Dimensional World on Earth 85
3. Get Rid of Vanity 87
4. Starting with Nothing, Empty-Handed 89
5. The Will of the Great Universe 91

What Is IRH?
The Institute for Research in Human Happiness
About the Author

Introduction

It is my pleasure to be able to publish this book, *The Starting Point of Happiness*, in which I have introduced ways that human beings can change, focusing on the concept of happiness. The book covers a wide range of topics, but the most important idea I wish to convey is that happiness is not something to get or take from others; instead it is what comes naturally when you have determined to bring happiness to yourself and to as many people as possible.

This basic idea is explained in a number of ways, such as "love that gives," "changing your perspective" and "exploration of the Right Mind." This book contains fragments of my essential philosophy. You will find them in every chapter.

Chapter 1 was originally published as a booklet of the same title, used for the elementary course of the Institute for Research in Human Happiness (IRH), which was established in 1986. Chapter 2, "On Love That Gives," originally appeared as a lecture based on the booklet. Chapters 3 through 8 were published in IRH's monthly magazine.

I have now compiled these texts to publish them in book form, as it is my wish to share my ideas with many who are not yet familiar with them. I am sure that each chapter could easily be expanded into a book. These short chapters, which summarize themes of deep significance, will serve for many readers as an introduction to my teachings of Truth.

I strongly believe that this book, containing the fundamental principles on which IRH is based, and important seeds of my thoughts, will inspire many readers. While it is intended mainly for newcomers, if you read and reread it carefully you will certainly attain a much higher level of understanding of Truth. It is my sincere hope that, with this book as an introduction to IRH, many readers will take a further step and join our group, to embark on a deeper study of Truth.

December 2000
Ryuho Okawa
President
The Institute for Research in Human Happiness

1: The Starting Point of Happiness

1. The Start of Your Life on Earth

You may sometimes find yourself seized by an indescribable fear and wish you could run away from reality. However, this is the very time to stand your ground and look back at how your life in this earthly world started.

You started with nothing. You may have been born rich or poor, but that made no difference to you as a baby, smiling innocently in your cradle. In a tiny body weighing about seven pounds, a little life was sleeping quietly, but with a strong determination to run the course in the race of life. Before you grew up to be an adult, you received so much care and gave so little back to others.

You may have experienced your very first setback as a small boy or girl when you compared your situation to that of others. Some people begin very early on to complain and become resentful. This is the way to drop out at the first lap of the race of life. Forgetting that they started out in this life with nothing and mistaking this earthly world for a permanent home, some people begin to compare what they have been given with what their friends have. As a result, they feel they have been given less than others and become discontented. A boy may envy his friend because the father is a wealthy doctor, his friend has plenty of money, and always wears expensive clothes. A girl may feel resentful because both her parents work during the day and do not have much time to spend with her.

However, everybody started out with nothing. In other words, we do not bring anything into this life with us. Starting with nothing, we are given so much in our childhood—clothes, food, a home, an allowance, educational opportunities, teachers, friends, materials for study, televisions, radios, stereos, and, above all, hope for the future. Starting with nothing and having been given a great deal, we nevertheless form an image of ourselves as needy.

If you reflect deeply, you will find that, even though you have grown up, the main cause of your anxiety has been comparing yourself with others. The roots of your suffering lie in your childhood, when you had already forgotten the starting point of your earthly life and begun to compare yourself and what you had with others around you.

Buddhism teaches the importance of knowing how to be content. Without the perception that every individual starts with nothing and lives a life that is unique, a life that cannot be compared with anyone else's, you will not understand this truth.

2. Discovering Your True Worth

We cannot remain children and keep comparing our situation with that of others. We each go through many different experiences, meet different people, and come across many different ideas. Then, at some point in our lives, an encounter with religious truth awaits. An encounter with Truth will bring you the powerful delight of discovery. Your true worth as a person lies not in the quantity of material wealth that has been gifted to you, nor in your reputation in the eyes of other people. Your true worth lies in the quality and the depth of Truth, the strength of the light that you can attain during this life on Earth. Awakening to this truth will completely turn your view of life around. You will realize that the more of your own divine nature you discover within yourself, the higher you will be able to rise spiritually.

3. Columbus's Egg

You may be familiar with the story of Columbus's egg. At a banquet to celebrate Columbus's discovery of the new continent, some criticized the explorer, saying that anyone could have discovered that land. Columbus then challenged those present to stand an egg up on the table. Everybody tried but failed. When his turn came finally, Columbus showed how to stand the egg up by making a crack in one end of the shell. This story illustrates how difficult it is to do something for the first time, even though it may look simple to everyone who comes after.

In a way, the truth about life is rather like the story of Columbus's egg. Great religious figures in the past have shown people how to stand an egg on one end again and again. They have shown that every one of us—we who start our earthly lives with nothing—has a possibility of becoming a saint if we continue to refine our souls, regardless of family background or upbringing.

What simple truth did these religious leaders show us, as Columbus did with his egg? They showed us that all we can take to the other world is our own souls. When we die, we have to leave our social status, our reputation, our property or other material possessions behind. If we return to the other world with only our souls, then the most valuable learning in this earthly world is to polish and refine our souls.

I imagine that many people will protest: "Anyone could have come up with such a simple truth." However, if no one had gone before to set an example, we would not be able to answer the question as to what human beings should learn from life. It is my sincere wish that as many people as possible awaken to the fact that the lives of great figures in the past are examples of Columbus's egg.

4. Refining Your Soul

Using the example of Columbus's egg, I have explained a truth about life. When you die and return to the other world, you cannot take anything with you except your soul. So concerns about anything other than your inner life will eventually come to naught. What distinguishes great figures from ordinary people is that they have awakened to the truth about refining their souls and have actually put that truth into practice. Unless you have made an effort to refine your soul you do not qualify to be called a great figure.

Abraham Lincoln is still widely respected, although there have been many presidents of the United States before and since. People respect him not because he reached the highest position in his country but because he continually refined his soul. "With malice toward none" was the motto he carried to the end of his life. Have you ever met anyone with the same motto as Lincoln, who makes the effort to put it into practice every day? Abraham Lincoln is very famous for his role in the American Civil War, as the man who succeeded in unifying north and south. Despite the fact that he represented the north, he told his wife and subordinates to stop speaking ill of southerners; he said they themselves would have behaved in the same way had they been born in the south. Lincoln continually refined his soul with mottos such as "with malice toward none, with charity for all" and "judge not, lest ye be judged." His attitude inspires hope.

Lincoln was born into a poor family, and he was said to have been not at all good looking. He was shot by John Wilkes Booth in Ford's Theater in Washington, D.C. on Friday, 14th April 1865, and died the next morning. Although he died a tragic death, in life he was filled with a golden light that inspired people all around the world. When Lincoln was on his deathbed in a cheap hotel room, his most trusted aide, Edwin M. Stanton, Secretary of War, murmured to himself that nobody in the world had such total control of his state of mind as the man who was lying there.

In fact, controlling our state of mind is the great challenge in life, and anyone can take up this challenge, anywhere, at any moment. When you are in complete command of your inner state, you will be one of those closest to God. When you have succeeded in solving the mysteries of the inner world, you will find a utopia within yourself.

5. Put Giving Love First

I have said that we start our lives with nothing and then grow up receiving a lot of help and love from the people around us, and if we do our best to refine our souls no matter what the circumstances, we can eventually become a man or woman of great character. We create our own worth ourselves. Our worth is not determined by our birth, our upbringing, or our experiences.

There are people who take too much interest in psychic abilities, who visit psychics to have readings about their past lives and then boast that they have been great figures in history. Even if it is true, it has no bearing on their present lives, nor does it throw any light on their future. Your worth right now depends on what you wish to achieve.

Do you continually complain about what you have been given and what is actually in front of you? Or do you know how to be grateful, and wish to give something back to society through your actions? It all depends which side you choose, giving or taking. In a way, this life is a trial, and we are all being tested every minute.

Think first about how you can give love and make this your daily goal. How much love can you give to people and society? Love is a blessing, an energy that nourishes others. Love is giving courage, strength, and hope to the people you meet in the course of your life.

Sooner or later you will realize that love is the will of God, and that it encourages every being to live and grow and create a great harmony. God's will is to encourage the development of every being. When you make up your mind to put the giving of love first, the light that comes from God fills you. When you start wishing to nourish others, compassion arises in you and this is the proof that you are the child of God.

There are two kinds of love—one is a love that takes, the other a love that gives. Love that takes is a synonym for attachment, while love that gives is the opposite of egotism and selfishness. Wanting to catch someone and control them completely, as you would catch a bird and keep it in a cage, is a far cry from love that gives. No matter how much money or how many things you give someone, if your aim is to bind them to you, it is a love that takes. True love is selfless. It does not expect anything in return, but encourages another person to grow and develop. Love does not bind another but finds goodness within and sets him or her free.

You have probably observed that the nature of love that gives is like the sun that constantly gives us light and heat, expecting nothing of us in return. In fact, another name for love that gives is compassion. Compassion is the very essence of love that gives, and it is the core of the will of God. Love that takes gives birth to a daughter called Jealousy, and a son called Self-Satisfaction. It does not give rise to happiness.

6. The Starting Point of Happiness

By now, you probably understand that happiness begins with the effort to put love that gives into practice. In other words, it is the effort of attuning to the compassion of God. When you determine to give love to the people around you and to society, letting go of your ego, that is your starting point of happiness.

If you cause others pain in the pursuit of your own satisfaction, you will never know the real meaning of happiness.

Let us make ourselves radiant in order to dispel the darkness and, like the flame of a candle, like a lighthouse, give out light to those around us. Even if a flame is passed from one torch to another, the flame of the original torch is not diminished. In the same way, the love that we give will spread and its sum will eventually light the darkness of the night, having been passed from one person to another, from one heart to another.

2: On Love That Gives

1. Starting with Nothing

In this chapter, I would like to enlarge on some main themes I discussed in the previous chapter. Let me begin by asking the question: "Why do people study Truth?" Perhaps none of you would have been attracted to the study of Truth had you not had some problem or purpose or dream of your own. I believe that each of you has certain goals and are endeavoring to attain them. Your decision to set out on this path may have meant new discoveries for you, a new angle of understanding, or an awakening in an area that is not directly connected to your current interests.

Studying the Truth requires making a constant effort to attain goals. We should not spend our time on Earth without any purpose, tossed about by worldly influences. If we live without purpose, it means that we are overlooking the real significance of this earthly life. This life is a precious opportunity that comes to us by the grace of God, and we must make the most of that opportunity.

Buddhism accepts the idea of reincarnation, the idea that we have many lives on Earth. Most of you have a three- or four-hundred-year period between each life. The majority of you were then born into this world with the aim of learning a great deal during the new lifetime, in a new environment and an unknown age. Unless you learn everything you can in this life, you are wasting precious time, for each incarnation is such a rare opportunity.

For you to be born into this world, a certain set of conditions had to be satisfied. You were born into the circumstances and times that best suited the purpose of your spiritual development. You have probably read books of philosophy and literature, and come across ideas about life such as, "human beings are born into this world at random" or "we have no choice about who our parents are, we just happened to be born to those parents and are compelled to live out random lives." This philosophy, known as existentialism, is quite plainly wrong. We are never thrown into this world accidentally; we always set up a purpose and a mission for each lifetime before we are born. We must abandon any ideas that life is merely accidental and replace them with a new perspective on life. Because it is an undeniable spiritual truth that we were born onto this Earth with a purpose and a mission.

Some people think they were born into this world completely accidentally, without any choice about their parents or their circumstances. Others believe that their circumstances are the result of their choices, and are those best suited for refining their souls. Depending on which attitude you adopt, your life will have a different significance, and many people do not understand that everything hinges on the choices that the individual makes.

We must remember that we were born on this Earth of our own free will. But in this case "free will" means that, with the guidance of higher spirits, we made the best choices for the purpose of refining our souls. Although the environment you now live in may not seem the best for you, it was the result of your choices, in conjunction with the recommendations of your guiding spirits.

As a person gifted with the ability to contact spiritual beings in the other world, I often have the chance to talk with them. I am constantly surprised by the differences in their levels of spiritual awakening. The words of higher spirits can nourish the souls of those who live on Earth. In contrast, there are some spirits who are unable to say anything valuable, and only grumble or moan.

When these spirits were living on Earth, they could probably communicate quite well with one another regardless of their spiritual levels. However, once they return to the other world, beings of different levels must go completely different ways. This happens because, in the spirit world, what a person thinks about or prays for most strongly reveals their true nature. Awakening to this truth will completely turn your view of life around. You will realize that the more of your own divine nature you discover within yourself, the higher you will be able to rise spiritually.

My conversations with spiritual beings always confirm that this world was created as a training ground for souls. Whether or not you accept this truth will greatly affect the course of your life.

Let me emphasize that no matter what experiences you may have had in previous lives, every time you are born into this world, you start with nothing. No matter what kind of spiritual discipline you have undergone, no matter what kind of realms you inhabited in the other world, when you were born as a baby into this world, you had to start anew, with nothing. This is the secret of life.

2. The Joy of Discovery

How do you feel about having to start out in life with nothing? Do you think this is fair or unfair? I would like you to reflect on this. I have made it clear that in IRH, worldly values do not affect a person's worth. Your social status, fame, wealth, educational background, age, or sex do not matter at all. The only criterion for respect at the Institute is the level of enlightenment you have attained. The higher the level of enlightenment, the greater the influence you will have; this is our basic policy and there is nothing strange in it.

When we started our lives in a physical body we were all equal in the sense that every one of us had to start with nothing. In this lifetime, we undergo a very severe spiritual discipline; because our achievements from past lives are not taken into account we must start anew. Everyone must start afresh, whether they suffered in hell for hundreds of years and were finally born into this world again, or whether they were the inhabitants of higher dimensions in the other world, such as Bosatsu* or Nyorai*. They must equally start afresh, from exactly the same starting line.

To start with nothing may seem a severe training, but if you ponder this deeply, you will see that it provides the best opportunities for your spiritual development. At birth, if you were to retain memories from past lives when you were kings, great religious leaders, or eminent scholars, how much would these contribute to the refinement of your soul in this lifetime? I am sure that they would only be a great burden to you.

If you are interested in the natural sciences, I would guess that you study something like physics, engineering, or electronics. Had you retained the memory of a past life as a great scientist like Newton or Archimedes, and had your parents continually reminded you of this past life, what would the present be like? It would be a life lived under great pressure to duplicate those achievements. In a way, it is a great mercy that we are given the opportunity to start each life on Earth with a clean slate.

Now I preside over IRH, give public lectures, and write books of Truth. But it was not until I was more than twenty years old that I even vaguely understood my true mission in this life. When I ask myself whether or not this was a good thing, I think it was fortunate. Completely unaware of my true mission, I lived an ordinary life, then I gradually came to feel my true self emerging. This brought me great joy.

Life is like a treasure-hunt. If you were told beforehand where the treasure was buried, there would be no excitement. As you look for hidden treasure on the journey of life, you can make great discoveries and find great joy.

*Note: There is a multi-dimensional structure in the other world. A Bosatsu is an inhabitant of the seventh dimension, while a Nyorai belongs to the eighth dimension. For details, refer to my book, *The Laws of Eternity*.

3. Reflecting on Yourself

Having recognized that we started our lives with nothing, we should remember to come back to this fact every day, as our starting point. Perhaps you have had many experiences in this world—at school, at home, or at work. Sometimes, others may have appreciated you, sometimes not. However, no matter what you experienced in this life, you were originally born with nothing, and there was little to distinguish you from other babies. Although you may have been slightly lighter or heavier than some of the others, there was no telling how each baby would turn out or what kind of person it would grow into. If you imagine hundreds of babies lined up in front of you, you would not be able to tell what kind of life each baby was going to lead. Each baby will have a unique life, depending on how it thinks, what it wishes for, and how it acts as it grows up.

When we come into this world, our guardian and guiding spirits, and angels in heaven are filled with hope and expectation, as well as great concern about our future. We sometimes see a baby that is alone smiling innocently. Sometimes there may be a mysterious expression on its face that parents cannot understand. Actually, in many such cases, because its heart is so pure, a baby can often see and respond to angels and other spiritual beings.

However, as children get used to this earthly world, they forget about the world of spirits and lose their ability to communicate with it. They start to make the mistake of thinking that this world on Earth is the only world that exists. As they reach school age, children begin to become concerned about the clothes they wear and whether or not their family is rich. As a result, some of them nurse discontent and resentment. Already, these children have forgotten that they started out in this life with nothing, and have begun to misunderstand this world seeing it as their only home.

If you are anxious at present, I would like to suggest that you reflect on the original cause of your current distress and see whether you can trace it back to your childhood when you began comparing yourself with others. Those who are prone to unhappiness always attribute their misery to outside circumstances, to external factors such as their birth, their upbringing, or those around them, accentuating their desire for what they are lacking. As they grow up, their agitation of mind will tend to increase rather than decrease.

4. Changing Your Perspective

It is so important to reflect on ourselves once in a while, and look back at the starting point of our lives, when we started out with nothing. Let us look at the example of a man who works for a famous and prestigious company. Viewed from the outside, he appears to be in very privileged circumstances, but he has got used to this and takes his excellent situation for granted. He then starts to focus on how he is treated, compared to his colleagues. If he sees that one colleague is more competent, or is being treated better than he is, he will become dissatisfied and start to complain. However, from a broader perspective, his situation is so much better than that of the average person. If you cannot look at your circumstances objectively, if you forget that when you started out in this life you had nothing, your suffering will only increase. I would like you to understand that pain and suffering arise out of comparing yourself with others.

In adulthood the course of your life will change, according to which way you focus. If you choose to compete against others or see everything in terms of superiority and inferiority, your life will be filled with pain. However, if you see relationships with others from the perspective that they involve a process of mutual refinement for higher ideals, this will bring you great blessings. If you are unsettled by the presence of those who had what you did not, or who enjoyed circumstances which were better than yours, it means that you have not yet discovered your true self.

Since I discovered my true self, I began to see the worth of many different people. I became joyful because I could appreciate that other people were wonderful; it meant that my soul had made great progress. I am proud that I have developed this ability to recognize the strengths of others, while maintaining my own peace of mind.

With a willingness to find the good in others, there is the promise of unlimited development. If you think that you have nothing to learn from others, or that nobody else's ideas are as good as yours, you are condemning yourself to a lonely life, and you will develop an unsociable character. If, on the other hand, you are willing to learn from the positive traits you can see in others, it means that the more excellent people there are in this world, the more examples there are for you to follow.

If you meet someone who appears to be enjoying better circumstances than you, see if you can simply admit that it is wonderful, or feel grateful that there are people in this world who are happy. If you are able to do this, you are moving successfully beyond the boundaries of mediocrity. If you just feel miserable when you see someone whose circumstances are better than your own, you have not taken even a single step toward enlightenment. Please understand this.

Always remember that you started out with nothing. Return to this starting point and look back at your life up to now. I hope that you can feel a sense of satisfaction at your achievements so far, and thankfulness for the people who have helped you. If you cannot, you have not yet awakened. If you complain that people always speak ill of you or that no one loved you or was kind to you, then there are scales covering your eyes and your view is distorted. Once this distortion is corrected, you will see that you had completely the wrong idea. Both directly and indirectly, you have received the help and love of many people. I think that the very fact you are living now is the result of the help of many people.

This understanding will awaken in you the truth about knowing how to be content. This does not mean that you have to remain as you are, or stop wishing for any further development. What I mean is that with a higher level of understanding, looking at things from a different perspective, you will see a completely new world open before you. Things you have ignored will stand out, as if they have been lit up. Without a complete change of perspective, it will be impossible for you to understand the true meaning of your life.

5. Finding Light in the Darkness

Starting with nothing and living out our lives on Earth, at some stage we reach the point where we discover our inner worth. At school, we may start to compare ourselves with others. At work, there will be plenty of opportunities to consider our relationships with others. Then, in due course, we will reach a point where we look to our inner self. For each person the timing is different, but sooner or later we come face to face with our innate tendencies, our karma, or the most important problem we have to solve in this life. It may be when we are in our twenties, thirties, fifties, or sixties. Exactly when this will happen is unpredictable, but at some point in this lifetime we cannot avoid confronting the problems assigned to us.

It may be through illness, a failure at work, a separation from family by death, a divorce, or something of that nature, but what has been deemed necessary for our spiritual discipline will inevitably happen at some point. This is the moment when we must face who we really are, stripped of the layers that have protected us. The self we have enclosed in a shell to keep safe and protected will be dragged out. At the hands of others or through our own actions, by a change in circumstances or times, we will be dragged from the incubator that has kept us warm and safe. We will be compelled to face ourselves, particularly the parts we most loathe seeing.

Life is not only happy and pleasant; it is also full of pain and sorrow. However, pain works as a whetstone on which we can refine ourselves, and sorrow gives the wish to understand our situation and can awaken our love for others. We have to acknowledge the existence of a system for refining our souls that has been carefully planned by God. Those who are spiritually advanced can continue to grow and reach higher levels of enlightenment while living a joyful life. However, those who do not wake up unless compelled by some critical problem will inevitably find themselves in adverse circumstances. Then an encounter with Truth awaits them.

An encounter with Truth will bring you the powerful delight of discovery. Your true worth as a person lies not in the quantity of material wealth that has been gifted to you, nor in your reputation in the eyes of other people. Your true worth lies in the quality and the depth of Truth, the strength of the light that you can attain during this life on Earth. (page 3)

The issue here is the quality of Truth you are able to discover, how deeply you can understand Truth, how strongly you can feel the light, and how much light you give out. It does not really matter what sort of experiences you have had or what sort of circumstances you have been placed in; simply ask yourself how strong a light you are emanating from where you are right now.

I would like to ask those who complain about their miserable circumstances or physical ailments: "How bright is the light you are giving out?" The faint glow of a firefly is almost invisible in the daytime, but gradually it becomes visible at dusk and then, at night, it becomes very clear. Similarly, the darker and more somber your life appears, the more brightly and clearly your inner light can be seen. So, if you think you are in deep darkness, determine to light a lamp to mark a new beginning, the light of your hope, the light of enlightenment. That light will gradually become clearer to your own eyes as well as to the eyes of others. In the future, when you look back, you will be proud of the great effort you made during difficult times.

6. The World Where Thought Is Everything

As a person who is gifted with spiritual abilities, I have the chance to speak with different orders of spiritual beings—with those who live in the heavenly realms and others who do not. I always find it sad that many spiritual beings have been reduced to miserable conditions in hell, despite the fact that they dressed decently and seemed to have done a reasonable job while they were alive. As I come across cases like this again and again, I have wondered why those who lived respectable lives have to suffer such misery, and through these experiences, I have come to feel strongly that as many people as possible must be taught a true perspective while they are still alive.

How can people who were able to have a reasonable conversation with one another while alive be reduced to beings who can do nothing but groan in suffering when they pass on to the other world? How awful, if such a future is awaiting us! It is terrible to be ignorant of what can happen in the future. I am quite sure you do not want to think that all the experiences in this lifetime could result in such misery. However, many people live out their lives in this world ignorant of spiritual truth, and although there is no such thing as "judgment," they will eventually have to take responsibility for their ignorance.

In the other world, thoughts manifest instantly, in contrast to this world where thoughts are invisible unless they are expressed or put into action. Often, ideas only materialize through the actions of others. However, in the other world, the Real World, nothing but thoughts exist. No matter how successfully someone pretends to be a lady or gentleman in this world, if they are filled with pain, sorrow, or harmful thoughts, what is within will manifest after they return to the other world.

The result will be an afterlife in a realm that corresponds to such thoughts.

In this world, the differences between people's states of mind do not seem very significant; but in the other world, the gaps are extremely wide. Each level is clearly differentiated. Like muddy water that is stirred and left to settle, it settles in layers—at the top the clear water, next the small particles, and, on the bottom, the layer where the sediment settles. According to the quality and quantity of the thoughts we have in this life, we will separate into different spiritual levels after the death of the body.

Once more I would like to call your attention to the importance of understanding this. In the spirit world, what you think and wish for most strongly make your true nature explicit. If you want to know who you are or to what kind of realm you belong, simply examine the contents of your mind during the day. The sum total of what you think each day will reveal your true nature and indicate to which level you will go when you pass over to the other world.

Once we awaken to this truth, it cannot but change our view of life completely. Indeed, the more of your own divine nature you discover within yourself, the higher you can rise spiritually. The next question, then, is how to live after this awakening.

7. Discovering a New Perspective

You are probably familiar with the discovery of the new continent by Christopher Columbus. In his time, it was not common knowledge that the Earth was round. Few people believed or supported the theory that it was possible to reach

India going west, although they knew it was possible to get there taking the eastern route. Columbus dared to believe the theory and sailed on. Actually, what he discovered was the West Indies, but undeniably it was he who opened the way for the discovery of a new continent.

Discovering the world of spirit is as momentous as the discovery of a new continent. But, unless people have been shown the way, they do not understand even simple truths. This applies in understanding spiritual truths. The world of spirit does exist—this is a simple truth. We live within the laws of reincarnation. This is a fact. Whether or not you accept it will make a major difference to the course of your life.

Regrettably, in modern education, these facts are ignored by the mainstream and there is not a widespread belief in the spirit world or in reincarnation. Those who blindly follow the prevailing ideas are like those people who said it was impossible to stand an egg up. I would like you think about your situation and ponder how you can make new discoveries about your present situation, about the education you received, about your workplace or your family life.

If you can look at your circumstances from a new angle, you will make new discoveries and find new principles for action in everyday life. Ask yourself: "If Columbus were in my place, what discoveries would he have made in my life? Up to now I have accepted and followed the ideas of the mainstream that most people take for granted, but could I not see things from a new perspective, or live in a completely different way?" The discoveries you make in daily life may be big or small, but I believe that each of you has the potential to stand the egg up, as Columbus did. I would suggest you think like this: "Many people will go on living ordinary lives just as I lived up to now, but if I were to look at things from a new and different standpoint, I could probably change my life."

This way of thinking applies to business management as well. If you own a business, what would you do in a time of economic recession? You might simply go along with the common argument that strong currency is detrimental to the exporting industry, and that it is impossible to make a profit in such an economic environment. This is like the people who tried to stand the egg up but failed. Another way of looking at the same situation is to see if you can find a way to make a profit because the currency is strong. In any situation there are always both positive and negative sides. So, if you ponder deeply and look for good ideas, you may have an unexpected breakthrough.

The same can be said of office work. After working for five or ten years in the same job you may find you have got into a rut with your work routine. When you were a newcomer you probably used to make a lot of discoveries, but it is likely that you have lost that initial enthusiasm. You may have come to feel that you know the job inside out, and that all you have to do is to be at the office from nine to five and then you can enjoy yourself after working hours.

Although you probably made many discoveries when you first started, you most likely become bound by traditions and fixed ideas. If you spoke out to offer an opinion or came up with an innovative idea, you may have been the target of criticism. As the years passed, you probably became less and less candid, and kept your opinions more and more to yourself, even when you made discoveries. In other words, you probably became conservative. This is how people who were originally capable of contributing something new may be held down, waste their own potential, and eventually be reduced to a state where payday is the only thing they look forward to anymore.

However, no matter what your situation, you can surely make new discoveries about your everyday life. Even if you have worked for ten or twenty years in the same job, it may be useful sometimes to imagine yourself as a newcomer again, and take a look at your present work situation through the eyes of that newcomer. No doubt you will find things that need to be changed, or areas of yourself you have neglected. Ask yourself why you have to do things the same way as others. There must be niches for new opportunities that no one has spotted yet. If you concentrate on looking for breakthroughs, you will certainly make unexpected discoveries.

8. Exploring Right Mind

At the Institute, we offer seminars and exams that motivate people to study. I could liken this system to Columbus's egg, because no other religious group has a similar educational system that involves examinations for members. At the beginning of our activities, many members were surprised by the fact they had to take exams. They could not believe that a religious group would give members scores, because in their minds religion was a place where people "licked one another's wounds" and consoled each other. This old way of thinking is like the attitude of those who said it was impossible to stand the egg up. However, at IRH we have a system whereby our members take examinations, at various levels, to test their knowledge of the Truth. I am sure that in the future other groups will follow suit, and imitate our style of education. I intend to continue to present innovative ideas like this at the Institute, and I am sure that each one of you, too, can make new discoveries in your own daily life.

Looking back through history, the geniuses and those who achieved great things were the ones who first set an example, just as Columbus did by sailing to the edge of the world. Millions of people were living as contemporaries of the great historical figures, but the difference between the genius and the ordinary person was whether or not that person was able to find a new perspective on common, everyday objects like an egg and how to stand it up—in other words, do something innovative in circumstances that were universally shared. Indeed, millions of people shared the same environment, and great historical figures did not have the privilege of possessing magic weapons; they used ordinary materials to produce extraordinary results. In the end, they proved that, regardless of family background or upbringing, anybody can become a great figure by refining their soul, even if they started out with nothing. If you look at the lives of great historical figures, you will notice that few come from privileged backgrounds; most had to go through difficulties before they reached their hour of glory.

What was the secret alchemy that turned lead to gold? The answer lies in the simple fact that these great historical figures were continually refining their own souls. This is not at all surprising, because, as we have seen, when we return to the other world we can take only our souls with us. At present, you may identify yourself with your physical body, but you are not your body. Even without a brain you can think. In fact, in the other world, spiritual beings do not have brains, but they still have thoughts. The brain is simply a machine.

If all you can take with you to the other world is your soul, what could be more important than refining it? Understanding this will inevitably change your ideas about what constitutes happiness in everyday life. Some of you may feel happy if you get a five-thousand-dollar increase in your annual salary, or if you can buy a new car at a bargain price. However, you cannot take the money or the car with you to the other world. This kind of happiness is shallow and temporary. The truth is so simple, but it is difficult to practice, and unfortunately most people do not notice that life is all about refining the soul. Actually, the majority of people have never thought seriously about their inner world.

At IRH, I teach how to refine the state of your mind, with the motto, "Exploration of Right Mind." This may sound simple, but many people are unable to put it into practice. Is there anyone you know who practices exploration of Right Mind? Among your colleagues, family members, or friends, is there anybody who focuses on the rightness of their thoughts? This is the secret of success in life.

The golden path to becoming one of life's winners is the exploration of Right Mind every day. The difference between those who continually explore the right state of mind and those who live aimlessly will become very evident in decades to come. After they leave this world, many people will have to spend a long time reflecting on their whole life and "settle up" for what they have done. Making a daily effort to attain Right Mind means reflecting thoroughly on your life so far, balancing up and settling your "account" every day. If you continue this practice of self-reflection each day, when your last day comes, you will have finished balancing the accounts for your whole life. Because you will know exactly what was right and what was wrong in your thoughts and actions, and because you have made adjustments and corrections to your inner life, you will be able to make rapid progress in spiritual learning in the other world.

9. The Watershed of Life

"Refining Your Soul" (page 4) focuses on the story of Abraham Lincoln. You must be familiar with the name "Lincoln" and an outline of his achievements. Of the many presidents of the United States, why is Lincoln so respected by people, not only in America but all over the world? I do not think the reason lies solely in his achievements.

Throughout history, there have been many people who achieved, in a worldly sense, as much as Lincoln. However, of the many military and political heroes in numerous countries, what made Lincoln outstanding was the principle he lived by, and which I mentioned earlier: "With malice toward none."

When I lived in the United States, I read a biography of Lincoln. The title, *With Malice Toward None*, was sufficient to reveal that this was a story about Lincoln, because he was the only person in American history known to have lived his life according to this principle. I therefore asked the question:

> Have you ever met anyone with the same motto as Lincoln, who makes the effort to put it into practice every day? (page 5)

It is extremely difficult to find anyone who lives by such a motto. In fact, it is so rare that the probability of finding someone would be less than one in a million. To have the intention not to harm others sounds so simple, but almost no one is able to put this into practice. Lincoln was a rare exception.

However, Lincoln's temperament was originally far from the calm suggested by the motto that was his guide in later years. As a young man, he was quick-tempered and got into many fights. According to his biography, early on in his career as a lawyer, he publicly criticized and argued with many people. One day, after he had launched an attack on someone, Lincoln was challenged to a duel. He had no choice but to accept the challenge, and was forced to fight. On a riverbank, back to back with his opponent, he started to count his paces, a weapon in hand, when suddenly a mediator stepped in and stopped the duel. He was saved. With this narrow escape from death, Lincoln learned a hard lesson—that too harsh a criticism of others can have very serious consequences. As a result of this shock, his views on life underwent a complete turnaround. He realized that it was easy to criticize and condemn others, but very difficult to live without harboring harmful thoughts toward any other human being. He decided to choose the difficult way.

We can easily find fault with others and point out their shortcomings or express our anger with them. However, it is extremely difficult to be tolerant enough to accept and forgive others' faults and to be kind toward them. The difference between someone who is ordinary and someone who is great lies in whether or not they can choose the difficult way.

Before his experience of the duel, Lincoln was quite ordinary. He was one of any number of people born into poor families, who worked very hard to make their way up to become successful politicians, lawyers, or professionals of some sort. After the duel, his views of life changed completely. From that time forward, he focused on putting into practice principles such as "with malice toward none, with charity for all," and "judge not, lest ye be judged."

Even during the Civil War, when his men and officers spoke ill of the southerners, he said: "We would be like them if the situation were reversed, so you are better not to speak ill of them." Can you think of any other commander-in-chief who made such generous comments about the enemy while engaged in fighting against them? In this respect, he was extraordinary. He knew that there are problems that have to be solved in a practical way, distinguishing right from wrong, but also that there is a higher perspective that embraces the whole.

You may be confronted with a similar situation. For example, suppose that a very nice man makes an error at work, and you are in a position to point out the mistake to him. Your attitude toward him makes a great difference—whether, with an understanding of his personality and his circumstances, you point out what was wrong from an awareness that it will be helpful to him to do so, or whether you simply vent your own frustration, without caring about him as a person. Viewed from the outside, there may not seem to be much difference in these two ways of acting, but we have to be aware of the difference, in terms of the mental attitude involved. Actually, the attitude we choose in each situation will affect our life from that point on. Such decisions are watersheds in our lives.

10. Toward Love That Does
Not Expect Anything in Return

Let us now take a look at the conclusion of Chapter 1 (page 6). At the risk of seeming redundant, let me say once again that starting with nothing, we grew up receiving a great deal of love and care from many people, but that we often forget this. The secret of success in this life is the truth that, no matter what our circumstances, we can become men and women of total integrity if we do our utmost to refine our souls.

The most important point is that your worth right now depends on what you wish to achieve. You may regret things in your past, but what is most important now is what you are going to do, what you are going to think, what you are going to express through your actions, and what you discover from now on.

> Do you continually complain about what you have been given and what is actually in front of you, as the result of the help of so many people? Or do you know how to be grateful, and do you wish to give something back to society through your actions? It all depends which you choose, giving or taking. In a way, this life is a trial, and we are all being tested every minute. (page 6)

No matter whether you choose to give or to take, your circumstances may appear outwardly unchanged. However, it is your attitude to your circumstances that will determine whether your inner world is colored by happiness or unhappiness. Happiness and unhappiness hinge on just one decision—how you control your mental attitude, how you approach other people and circumstances.

It is impossible to control another person's thoughts or feelings. Although we can influence others, we cannot change them, because each person has their own free will. The free will of each individual is firmly established and protected. However, if we apply this principle of free will to ourselves, we are perfectly able to change our own thoughts and attitudes. This is actually a great blessing. If we could effect only a fifty percent change in ourselves we would not only be able to take responsibility for our lives, but it would be as if we had been given the steering wheel of the car, so that we could steer our lives in the right direction. We are put in total charge of controlling our own thoughts. Herein lies the origin of our responsibility.

Let me suggest that first we start to give love, because whether we realize it or not, we have been given a lot of things, and the blessings of many people. We should not be content only to receive, but should also feel gratitude and express this through our wish to offer something in return.

> Love is a blessing, an energy that nourishes others. Love is giving courage, strength, and hope to the people you meet in the course of your life. (page 6)

I would like you to realize that love is the will of God. "Love that gives" is the principle that constitutes the very foundation of the teachings of Truth at the Institute. However, the majority of people in this world seem to confuse "love that gives" with "love that takes" or "love you feel entitled to." Until you change this mistaken idea about love, you will not be able to attain true peace of mind.

If you ponder deeply, I am sure you will remember all the many things that have been given to you by others. There are probably so many people who have helped you that you cannot count them all. On the other hand, can you recall what you have done for others? Try to make a balance sheet, putting "love you have been given" as a heading on one side, and "love you have given" on the other. In most cases, the liabilities will outweigh the assets. You will almost certainly be astonished by the enormous gap between them, and thus be motivated to reflect on your life.

When you contemplate love, be careful to remember that love that binds others and deprives them of their freedom is not "love that gives." This sort of misunderstanding is often seen in the love of parents for their children. There are many parents who complain that, although they have given so much to their children in bringing them up, their children are ungrateful. This problem appears to be universal. Ponder deeply as to whether what parents think is love is really "love that gives."

If you do something for another and expect something in return, love dies. Do you give your love in the same way that you would feed a bird, so that it will not fly away from the cage? Love is often misunderstood. Giving love and then expecting something in return is no different from the give-and-take basis of any commercial relationship. It is wrong to look at love in this way. If you cannot feel joy in the very act of giving love, what you think is love is not real.

One of the most significant characteristics of today's world is that many people exhibit a love that binds instead of love that gives. Love that binds others is not really love, but an expression of egotism that aims to catch and control another.

Unfortunately, many people do not understand this point, and it is my strong wish that you awaken to this Truth.

Ask yourself these questions: "Am I trying to control my child, my wife, or my husband? Is my true intention to bind my partner to me? Even though I feel I am taking good care of my staff, am I trying to control them?"

True love is selfless. It does not bind others but finds the goodness within and sets them free. Remember this always, and reflect on yourself in the light of it. Then you will understand that "love that gives" is a synonym for compassion, the selfless love of God.

11. What Is the Starting Point of Happiness?

What is the starting point of happiness? You will find the answer when you decide to give love to other people and to society, setting aside your egotistical desires. Imagine the flame of a single candle that has the power to light tens of thousands of candles. You strike a match and light one candle, and that flame can spread to hundreds, thousands, even millions of other candles.

The essence of love that gives is like the flame of that candle. If you let your inner light shine through, it will set others alight. Like the flame of the first candle that does not diminish when it lights others, love is inexhaustible. The more love you give, the more love increases. Keeping this in mind, make the effort to become the first flame that will light other candles, other torches. Remember, your inner happiness can lead others to happiness. This idea lies at the heart of the teachings of Truth at IRH.

3: Embark on the Journey to Bring Happiness to the Whole of Mankind

1. The Discovery of a Great Love

In this chapter, I would like to explain some of the basic principles on which the Institute for Research in Human Happiness is based. Over and over again, I have stressed the importance of building solid foundations: "First, build the base before erecting columns"; "First consolidate the inside before expanding." These were the slogans I used to convey to members. In my open lectures, too, I actually said that, at the early stages of the activities of the Institute, I wanted to concentrate on creating a solid base. So I preferred to limit the number of members to ensure a certain standard of learning.

Having built a solid foundation, you will start your activities, and the most important theme in this process will be the discovery of a great love. From ancient times, love has been talked of in a variety of ways, and you will probably accept without question that love is a wonderful thing. I would like to investigate the idea of love, a love that involves not only the love that exists between human beings but also a higher love. I would like you to ponder the love of God, a sacred love that manifests divine light.

In actual fact, love takes many different forms. Although it is not visible, love travels around the world—through the hearts and minds of the people who live in it—as if it were the blood circulating within God. It is important to discover this great love. It means being awake to the fact that while we live through the endless cycles of reincarnation, we are being allowed in this particular era, at the beginning of the 21st century, to live in the presence of love.

We usually take it for granted that we are living at this time on Earth with the people around us, but we need to be aware of how great a privilege it is to be allowed to enjoy this era. The ability to perceive the presence of love is important, and discovering that we are being allowed to live through the great love of God will become the basis for a new principle of action. This awareness is the starting point of gratitude, and then the next step is to respond to the favor that has been given to us. Having become aware of the great love, or having discovered it, we are then expected to translate it into our own acts of love, and to express love in our relationships with other people.

It is not enough to find love in the hearts of others or in our own heart. We should aim to discover the workings of God, to see how the hand of God is expressed as love. Starting from an awareness of the great love by which we have been granted a life on planet Earth at this time, when Truth is being taught, I wish to suggest a new set of principles for action.

2. The Advance of Light

When each one of us lives each day to the full, as an envoy of light, refining ourselves and giving out light, the sum total of each person's effort creates a great advance of light. So, when we consider a set of principles to guide our activities, we should ensure that the track we leave behind us does actually give out light.

As travelers walking on the path of light, what should we aim for? What kind of vision should we hold? What should we expect? In considering these questions, we must remember that this journey is not just to benefit ourselves. The destination is the edifice where God dwells, and we are to walk the wide and sacred road that leads there. Before us opens a long straight road, and we must continue to walk on it, without stopping or retreating.

However, human beings can easily be swayed by selfish desires, by wanting to realize one's own small hopes and wishes. We can easily become attached to manifesting our personal goals. The term "self-realization" can imply the realization of a magnificent vision, or the meaning can be limited to the bringing of our personal desires into reality. If this term is used to imply the manifesting of selfish desires, the original meaning becomes extremely narrow. When we consider our journey as a journey of light, we must not be attached to narrow personal goals, but instead aim to realize the great goal.

Now, what kind of self-realization will create a journey of light? As I have repeatedly taught at IRH, it is realizing one's desire to serve God, as an instrument. We should never, ever forget this. In the future, some of you may become lecturers or leaders of our local churches. Even if this happens, do not ever think you have become exalted, but remain humble, and have the strong desire to work as an instrument of God, to be one of his fingertips.

Actually, those who can be called "angels of light" have started to gather at the Institute. However, even if you become aware you are one of them, you should not be arrogant or haughty. The more acute your awareness that you are an angel of light becomes, the more humble you must be. The more blessed you are, the more is required of you in serving God.

If you are concerned about your position relative to other people, be it higher or lower, remember that you are not helping God. I would like to remind those of you who will be future leaders of this. Do not think that because you are a leader you are exalted; do not forget you are a volunteer, serving to help create the great advance of God's light.

3. Keep on Advancing, Never Retreat
Once we embark on the great path of taking part in realizing God's will, and embraced by his great compassion, all of our actions should reflect this commitment. There is no uncertainty in this, and there should be no hesitation.

Advance, only advance on this path. When all ambiguity is cleared away, there is no other way to go except straight forward. On the way, you may encounter difficulties and obstacles, or meet people who do not accept you. However, you should not try to argue with such people, or criticize them. Nor is there any need to conclude that they are mistaken simply because they do not agree with you at this moment.

We form a great river of love. We are each a part of this river that flows with tremendous force. No matter what kind of obstacles await, whether they be dams or rocks or fallen trees in the way, the torrent just flows over them and keeps on advancing. Like wild water that pushes forward through any obstacle and carries on all the way to the sea, let us advance forcefully, as a great river of love and as a torrent of positive intentions.

There is no room for excuses that we cannot advance because of obstructions. We need to overcome obstacles, and if they sometimes seem insurmountable, we must learn how to pass beneath them or even bypass them. In this way, when we move forward as a torrent of love, there will be no evil or enemies to bar our way. Enemies come into being from a perspective that distinguishes ourselves from others; in other words from the feeling of separation. From the perspective of the absolute, love has no enemies. When the positive energy of love embraces all beings, enemies or evil will cease to exist.

If you find yourself faced with opponents, you have to understand that you do not have sufficient love. If you ever come across someone who appears to oppose you, you need to know your love is not deep enough. If we are to embrace all people with a far greater love, like God's love, we should know that there is no evil or enemy. On the basis of this grand perspective, let us keep going forward.

4. Time to Transcend the Barrier between Self and Others

Another important idea we should remember is transcending the barrier that separates the "self" and "others." The fact that you have been born on this Earth in this current age means that each and every one of you has a great mission. There is no question about this. You have all been entrusted with a great mission.

One important thing I would like you to know is that you should not see yourself as separate from other people. In the heavenly world, too, there are differences. There are higher spirits who have a variety of different personalities and diverse philosophies and ideas. Although these differences arise out of the variety of individuality, the purpose of this diversity of character is to merge together and create a great work of light, not to criticize or repel one another. That is the reason that it is important to strive to transcend the differences between yourself and others through the practice of love, through loving actions, and the advance of your love.

I would like you to consider deeply how you can climb over the wall that exists between you and others. Reflect on yourself daily to examine what was in your mind during the day, whether you were thinking only of your own interests. Check to see whether you were preoccupied with your personal happiness or unhappiness. I would like you to see whether the phrases that come into your mind begin with "I" or "my."

One of the most important ideas of Buddhism—the three seals of the Dharma—is egolessness; it implies that God's law governs the whole universe without any hindrance. It permeates the entire universe, without any obstructions. His energy, the energy of love, circulates through the universe without obstacle.

With this truth in mind, those of you who find yourselves always preoccupied with your own interests, constantly comparing yourselves to others, or who tend to criticize others must reconsider your way of being. Those who have developed an advanced state of mind can experience moments when the day passes beautifully, without them thinking about themselves. I would like you to treasure such moments that pass lucidly, like a clear stream of water that keeps flowing.

5. Seven Declarations for Happiness

To conclude this chapter, I would like to make seven declarations for happiness. The purpose of these are, needless to say, to bring happiness to the whole of mankind as well as to the individual. They will serve as a flag to lead our advance of light. The following are the seven declarations:

1st Declaration: Exploration of Truth

For the happiness of humanity, we shall strive towards the goal of exploring Truth thoroughly and deeply.

2nd Declaration: Study of Truth

For the happiness of humanity, we hereby pledge to study Truth thoroughly and deeply.

3rd Declaration: Conveying Truth

We hereby pledge to devote all our energy to the conveying of Truth to many.

4th Declaration: Actualization of Love

We hereby pledge to discover the great love, and to live every day actualizing it in our daily lives.

5th Declaration: Creation of Happiness

We shall be engaged in the actual practice of creating happiness, not only for those who are now living, but also for those who will come after.

6th Declaration: Development of Humanity

Our overall goal is the development of humanity as a whole.

7th Declaration: Creation of Utopia on Earth

Our ultimate goal is to create a utopia on Earth, and transform the heavenly world of the fourth dimension and above into an ideal world. In other words, we shall strive to change the entire world that was created by God into utopia.

Using what I have said so far as your guidelines, I would like you to continue advancing. I, myself, will devote all my time and energy to realizing our great goal; I would like you, too, to consider carefully what kind of contribution you can make, using the time that is allotted to you. Do not be content just to listen to others, or sharing experiences that have touched your soul with them, but consider carefully how you yourself can explain the experiences you have had that have kindled your soul, and share your knowledge with others. I would like you to continue advancing, starting from the determination to explore Right Mind and to continue practicing the Principles of Happiness, steadily following the three steps of first exploring Truth, studying Truth, and conveying Truth to others.

4: The Starting Point of Faith

1. An Encounter with God

In this chapter, I would like to talk about faith. An important theme in any discussion on faith is an encounter with God. This encounter is the most solemn moment, the holiest moment of your life.

From the time you were a small child, you probably came across religious objects such as statues of Jesus on the cross or statues of Buddha. Up to now, you may have thought that religion dealt with what exists outside you, outside your window, outside the curtains.

However, at some point in our lives, we are all given the chance to encounter God. It may be through the experience of failure or a major setback; the clue may be a serious illness, disappointment in finding a job or in love, or perhaps a marriage that ends in divorce. All these experiences may seem setbacks on the journey of life, in the process of refining ourselves, but these are also the moments that allow us to reflect deeply, the moments when we turn to God.

Difficulties and problems, failures and setbacks are usually seen as negative. But it is not entirely right to see them in this way. In failure, you find also the seeds of success; in sorrow, the seeds of joy. I really think it is important to look at these apparent setbacks in a different way.

People who simplistically see the world from a perspective of duality—in other words, people who judge situations to be good or bad—would probably say: "If God exists, why is the world so full of distress and sorrow?" They wonder why there is so much misery and hardship in people's lives, why they have to experience the pain of facing death, of separation from loved ones, or of poverty.

Life is full of pain and sorrow, but these do not exist for their own sake. In fact, what appears to be pain or sorrow is often an expression of God's love in disguise. In Buddhism, sufferings in life are sometimes described as the expedient measures to lead people to enlightenment. Trials are like a whetstone that polishes our souls, and through our trials an encounter with God awaits.

If everything went smoothly and you had no serious problems in your life—if, as a child, you grew up healthy, did well at school, graduated from a reasonably good university, found a respectable job, married happily and enjoyed a good family life, then grew old and eventually died peacefully—you would probably have little chance of experiencing the ultimate encounter. However, in reality, at some point in life, everybody experiences failure of some kind, and everybody experiences sleepless nights. You probably lost your appetite after a painful experience, or spent sleepless nights in pain or in a state of anxiety.

The question, then, is how you see life's difficulties, how you assess them, and how you react to them. Faced with difficulty or pain, anxiety or suffering, do you see these as a manifestation of evil? Do you curse the world, heaven, and other people, or can you perceive in difficulties the prompting to become a better person? Can you see them as an expression of the love of God? These are two different ways of seeing the same circumstances.

You may have experienced pain or sorrow, as well as unexpected success. At a time when you least expected it, you may have had the joy of meeting your future spouse, or perhaps after a long period of unfulfilled hope, you experienced the delight of the arrival of a baby. After you had almost given up hope of being promoted in your job, you may have had the pleasant surprise of being chosen for a top position. These unexpected and almost unbelievable successes also bring with them the chance to encounter God, for in such moments of joy, we want to express our gratitude to the power that has brought us success.

Life is full of opportunities to encounter God, but many people are not sensitive enough to notice these moments. It is my sincere wish that in times of both suffering and joy, you will have the good fortune to encounter Him. This is your first step to a higher perspective on life.

2. Be Pure in Heart

You may wonder how it is possible to encounter the supreme consciousness through the various experiences of your life. In the Bible, there is a sentence from the Sermon on the Mount that clearly explains the way to encounter God: "Blessed are the pure in heart, for they shall see God." (Matt. 5:8) This phrase has long been a source of comfort to Christians. For two thousand years they have believed these words of Jesus Christ, and made an effort to be pure in heart, so that they might indeed see God.

"Blessed are the pure in heart, for they shall see God." This is very simple, but it is such an important message. I am teaching that by reflecting on your thoughts and making them pure, you can remove the impurities that overshadow your soul. Then you will be filled with the light of heaven, and you can attune yourself to the vibrations of the heavenly world. When you can do this, you will be able to communicate with your guardian and guiding spirits. This method is absolutely correct, and the state of mind you will experience as a result of this practice was actually taught by Jesus Christ two thousand years ago in Israel.

"Blessed are the pure in heart, for they shall see God." Jesus was right. At the Institute, I teach self-reflective meditation to achieve this same goal. How can we become pure in heart? By bringing wrong thoughts back on track. If you have thoughts that would not please Him, you should reflect on and correct them; if you have done something wrong, ask forgiveness and feel truly sorry for your wrongdoing.

Human beings are prone to making errors and mistakes, but this does not give us the excuse to do nothing, for fear of making mistakes. Because we are apt to make mistakes, we should seek a right way of living through self-reflection, and with the aid of prayer we should try to correct our wrong thoughts and deeds. As you make an effort to live in the right way, remember Jesus' words: "Blessed are the pure in heart, for they shall see God."

In today's world, many people seem to be living in accordance with their personal views of life. I wonder how many can see the value of being pure in heart. I guess not even one in a hundred. If you were to ask people in the street: "Are you making an effort to live with a pure heart?" it is very unlikely that you would hear any of them answer "yes." On a Sunday, if you were to stop a Christian on their way home from church, the probability might be higher, but once back into everyday life, it is easy to forget this ideal.

I encourage you to be pure in heart, and to refine your mind. As you make an effort to live with a pure heart, you may have mysterious experiences, and come to feel the existence of God. You may witness miracles.

3. Fighting the Desire to Assert the Ego

I would like to explore the importance of being pure in heart from yet another angle. As members of IRH, your ultimate goal ought to be to become Bosatsu, or angels of light. It is true that this kind of self-recognition works to motivate you to climb, step by step, toward a higher objective. However, along the path, there is also the danger that this kind of understanding could trap and degrade you.

In the previous chapter, I talked about the danger of conceit, for it is the main reason that highly disciplined seekers go astray. If you are receiving the appreciation that you feel you deserve, the right attitude as a seeker is to accept that appreciation with humility, and resolve to continue to make even more effort to improve yourself. However, when people express appreciation for work, some recipients not only take this appreciation for granted, but expect even more praise. This reaction is typical of those who are conceited—the more they are given, the more they demand.

The more important your mission, the greater the responsibility you shoulder. The higher your position, the more carefully you should reflect on yourself, and the more humbly you should conduct yourself. In this way, you will be able to achieve great stature. Never be satisfied with small successes. Constantly fight against the desire to excessively assert yourself—the desire to appear better than you really are, or to show others how hard you work, or how wonderful you are.

However, the desire for success is one of the most basic human desires, and aspiring to success in a worthy cause is a form of desire. If humanity did not have ambitions to succeed, or aspirations to higher ideals, no civilization or culture could have flourished on Earth. However, the desire to attain higher ideals often gives rise to problems associated with over-assertiveness.

From the perspective of Truth, why is over-assertiveness a problem? It is worthwhile considering this question. The problem of excessive assertiveness is connected to the idea of relative standing. If in your mind you banish others to a lower position, this is because you feel your standing improves. Your delight at assuming a higher position can easily turn into the false pride of looking down on others. However, if the situation were reversed, you would be unhappy because you would have been deprived of your status.

If you are preoccupied with your position relative to others, you are a long way from a state of absolute happiness, from total devotion, and faith in God. Not only are you seeing yourself as completely unconnected to other people, but also you are not wishing others happiness. These are basic characteristics of people who have a burning desire to assert their selfish desires. Deep down, they do not want happiness for others, and they only crave admiration for themselves. Ultimately, they want to take love from others, and they are like spiritual vampires.

Giving love is the way to spiritual refinement, so if you are depriving others of love, you are not on the path to enlightenment. As a seeker, you should plant roses along your path instead of picking blooms that others have sown. To continue this analogy, those who are over-assertive seem to pick all the flowers that line the path, to decorate themselves and wear them in their lapels.

The right way of living based on Truth is to sow seeds, plant bulbs, and grow flowers where before there were none. Where you have sown seeds and planted bulbs, flowers will bloom after you have passed by. You may not be able to see the flowers yourself, and perhaps only those who come after will be able to enjoy them. However, the way of the seeker is to keep on sowing seeds and planting bulbs, even if others are unaware of your efforts. There is no desire to assert selfish desires. I would like you to consider whether you are attempting to pick flowers to adorn yourself, or whether you are making an effort to sow seeds for those who will come after.

4. Feelings of Inferiority and Love

Let us now explore the sense of inferiority that lies behind an excessive desire to assert the self. Everyone has feelings of inferiority of one sort or another, and there are two ways of reacting to these feelings. The first is, as a result of deep wounds, to become trapped in a vicious cycle that only brings more unhappiness. The second way is to use feelings of inferiority as a springboard to open a way through to the future, as do those who strive for feelings of completeness.

However, no matter which way people react, those who have an inferiority complex have unhealed wounds within, and they do not have peace of mind. Feelings of inferiority arise out of a sense that we have not been given enough. As a result, such people have a much stronger longing for love than people who do not have feelings of inferiority; love is the medicine that cures all illness, the spring that heals the wounds of every heart. This is the nature of love.

We can see that one important characteristic of love is that it treats every individual equally; it gives to everybody without discrimination. The essence of love is to find the light in everybody and everything, to appreciate and praise it. With love, you will be able to find something wondrous in tiny insects, in flowers, in all beings, and to cherish them all. With love, you will be able to find the divine nature that radiates light in every person.

Love functions to heal and erase feelings of inferiority that may come into being as we live out our Earthly lives. Love is the manifestation of the wish to give. As I have said repeatedly, the essence of love is to be found in continually giving, without expecting anything in return.

Those of you who suffer from a sense of inferiority are probably too occupied with the desire to receive love. If you think this applies to you, it is important to stop thinking about yourself, and reflect deeply on the importance of giving love without expecting anything in return. You should understand that thoughts such as "since I have worked so hard, I am entitled to receive the corresponding amount of appreciation," or "because I did so much for him, he should love me," reflect a wrong way of thinking.

The essence of love is to give continually, without expecting anything in return. It is to keep on sowing seeds and planting bulbs even if you yourself do not see them bloom. As you look around and see people suffering from feelings of inferiority, and if you discover that you, too, have these same feelings, you must understand how important it is to give love. You must open your eyes to the power of love to heal the wounds in other people's hearts. The deeper your feelings of inferiority, the more keenly you need to realize the idea that there is not enough love in this world.

Keep sowing seeds and planting bulbs for others to enjoy. As you continue to do this, you will understand that the essence of love lies in selfless acts that enrich others. Do not expect anything in return, because as soon as you expect some reward, the love you give will die. The moment you expect some return, the seeds you have sown and the bulbs you have planted will die. Never expect anything in return.

5. The Starting Point of Faith

I would like to conclude this chapter with some thoughts on the starting point of faith. Throughout the preceding discussion—of issues such as encountering God, being pure in heart, the desire to assert the self, and feelings of inferiority—my intention is to explain that the starting point of faith is to acknowledge that you are imperfect. If you think of yourself as infallible, and feel satisfied with yourself the way you are, you may have little chance of awakening to faith.

None of us is perfect. We are immature, we are full of shortcomings and faults. But a realization of our present state will lead us to a higher order of understanding. Because we are imperfect, we can continue to aim for high ideals. Here lies the force that awakens faith in us. The less perfect we find ourselves, the greater the awakening of our love for God who is perfect and flawless. He expresses Himself in ideals; so to love ideals is to love Him.

The starting point of faith is deep reflection on yourself, with humility, and in that humility you will find a path that will eventually reach God. Do not give up this goal, no matter how miserable or hopeless your situation seems to you, no matter how burdened you are by feelings of inferiority or anxiety. Despite all your faults, you are His creation, and your essential nature is no different from His. To have faith means to make the effort to move toward the great ideal of finding your True Self. To live a life of faith, it is essential to have ideals, and the ideals you hold should be the same as those of God.

Coming face to face with your own incompleteness will motivate you to aspire to completeness. This willingness is the driving force of faith; it gives the power to develop your own self and at the same time encourage others to grow.

As you continue to study Truth, I would like you to remember the starting point of faith, the starting point of the journey toward God, and to approach Him every day with steady steps. Be pure in heart, and be filled with love.

5: In Springtime

1. The Season of Endurance

When spring comes, a special brightness seems to permeate every field and mountain; everywhere, the singing of birds can be heard. It seems as if the season of spring comes to teach us about the breath of life, as well as the different seasons of human life. I wonder what people think of the fact that spring comes every year, without fail.

The fact that spring comes round every year and is never late reveals the great compassion of God. When I feel the breath of spring, I feel the breath of God's life. It is His nurturing of everything that is about to grow; it is His encouragement to those who are going to advance toward success.

In the springtime, I find that there is a source of courage and hope, that there is a wellspring of power. Here, I find a starting point for a great leap into the future. In the vibrant energy of spring that is granted to us by God's grace, we need to be able to appreciate the vitality of nature to the full.

However, this vibrant energy of spring does not come without any preparation. Before the spring there are always severe, cold winter months. Winter is the season of endurance. Likewise in our life we experience periods of endurance, but it is not just endurance for the sake of endurance. Suffering is not just for its own sake. It is only the backdrop to highlight the signs of spring.

I imagine that many of you who are reading this book are experiencing worries and sufferings of one sort or another or rather, that most of you have something to worry about. What is the origin of your worries? The basic reason for them is a lack of trust. Trust in what? It is because you lack trust in yourself, trust in other people, and trust in God that worries and troubles arise.

Now I would like to ask you some questions. Why do you always anticipate that something bad will happen? Why do you always think that you will fail? Why do you expect people to betray you? Why do you think that God always does things that go against your wishes? Why is it that you hold on to such a grim view of life, and so betray yourself and others, and God, too? How much happiness can this kind of gloomy perspective possibly bring you?

Even when you appear to others to be experiencing a season of endurance, or when you feel you are, it is often because you lack these three kinds of trust. If you could have complete trust, there would be nothing to worry about, and you would not suffer.

I would like to ask those who are experiencing pain these questions: Do you have trust in yourself? Do you trust others? Do you trust God? Perhaps you lack these three kinds of trust. In this case, you will need to reflect on yourself to become aware of your basic attitudes. When you do not trust yourself, do not trust those who you encounter on your journey of life and, above all, do not trust in God, how can you expect to attain happiness?

I would like you to develop a stronger trust in yourself. When you have these three types of trust, how could a bad situation arise? Even if you are confronted with a period of suffering, it may only be suffering because you do not believe that the vibrant season of spring awaits you. Do you ever think that people are in this world only to cause you harm? Do you ever believe that God exists to bring you punishment? Do you think you, yourself, have come into this world simply to fail? This cannot be the case.

If you are one of those people who think they are experiencing the harsh cold of winter, you need to reflect on your own attitudes, focusing on the three checkpoints. First, you need to start with a firm belief that you are the child of God. If this is true of you, it must also be true of others; they are also the children of God. He is watching over the world where His children are living together.

What are you worried about? Why do you worry that you may fall ill? Why do you anticipate financial difficulty? Why do you think people might make fun of you? Why can't you think that great honor and admiration await you, further down the line? When you lead your life in accordance with the will of God, there are no ordeals or suffering from a spiritual point of view. If you think you are faced with these sorts of difficulties, this is simply the result of your negative thinking. They are only illusions. The fact that you are lacking trust means that you have forgotten you are living in a world created by God, and that you just cannot believe in this truth.

Do you believe this world was created by God? If you do, then first you must believe in yourself, you who are a child of God, and you must also believe in other people who must also be His children. Above all, you must believe in Him. When you do, the season of endurance will come to an end and instead, a song of praise for His vital energy will arise with the breath of spring.

2. The Torrent of Life Force

I have said that a season of endurance is simply a time when trust is lacking. However, at the same time, we do not have to be content with an inactive state of simply trusting ourselves, trusting others and God. We must not remain in this state of passivity in which we just expect something good to happen.

When spring comes, see how merrily the birds sing, how happily the children play. Even the bees seem to sing. Dogs and cats seem happier, and the other animals look as if they are smiling. The grass and all the plants seem to be growing and full of vital energy. Why do the streams look so beautiful in the spring? Why do little fish seem to be swimming so merrily? All this is because the sunlight feels so warm in the springtime. The sunlight symbolizes life energy, the energy of compassion.

Nevertheless, we must not just wait for good news to come. When you think that you have reached the spring, then you need to join the great torrent of life energy and keep on pushing forward until you reach the sea. You need to live courageously amid the gushing life force.

In the season of endurance there is a period when you just have to wait, but eventually this period is over. Then, you need to know that the time has come when you have to make a decision and take action.

Earlier, I taught that when there is a time of confusion, you need to maintain the status quo. However, this does not mean you can remain indecisive. It means that instead of doing something ill-advised you need to wait for a while and accumulate energy within. When the spring comes, the cherry blossoms burst forth and all living beings start to move. I am saying that you should accumulate energy in the same way, quietly and steadily beneath the cover of snow.

Winter does not continue forever. Some day, it must end. You must not continue to hold on to the winter. You do not have to think about the snow all the time. When the spring comes, you should shed your winter coat. You have to take off your heavy jacket and change into spring attire. I am not only talking about your outer appearance, but also of your state of mind. Just as you shed your winter clothes and put on spring attire, why not get rid of your heavy burden and become light-hearted? Why not expect something wonderful to happen? Why do you think only about difficulties?

After the stage of maintaining the status quo comes the stage of making decisions and taking decisive action. Those who are indecisive are, after all, anticipating something bad will happen in the future and worrying in advance. The force that will destroy such unnecessary worries is the power of belief, the power of believing that the future will be full of hope. For those who believe a path will open, nothing is impossible. There are only possibilities. There will come a time when you have to stand up, and become like the towering giant who courageously cut a path with a golden axe in his hand. This is the springtime of your life.

First, look at yourself and try to see the potential for development that is growing within you, like buds that are about to burst. Even in winter, buds of flowers continue to grow silently but steadily. Under the cover of snow, the buds of the plum blossom keep on growing and getting ready to bloom. In the icy winds of winter, the cherry blossom buds are already starting to grow, weathering the chill. If trees can do this, then, in the same way, you need to accumulate sufficient energy within and allow the buds of development within you to grow before the season of unfolding actually begins.

You need to check whether sufficient energy is being stored to bring happiness to yourself and to the whole of mankind in the future. Check to see if you really are determined to turn this world into a utopia and whether you have stored enough energy to realize this great goal.

When an abundance of strength has accumulated within you, it will inevitably start to overflow. If buds have started shooting on the branches of a tree, they will continue to grow, and in time they will come to full bloom. When the right time comes, what will happen will happen.

Before the time of unfolding, prepare sufficiently within yourself. When you see the buds of flowers are shooting forth, make sure you encourage them to grow bigger. When they start to open, first make sure that they come to quarter bloom, then bring them to half bloom, and finally to full bloom. In this way, walk the path of development courageously, step by step, in high spirits.

3. The Presence of Infinite Wisdom

I would like to tell you something that I am sure will encourage you—each and every one of us has a golden channel that leads to God. We experience affliction and sadness because we think that each human being is an isolated individual; that we are unrelated to one another and drift aimlessly like grass floating on water. However, when we become aware that there is a golden pipeline within each one of us that stretches to infinity and to the realm of God, then all fear should melt away.

Do not expect anything from others or from your environment. Do not expect others to do things for you, or expect your surroundings to change to your advantage. Instead, look within and attempt to discover the golden channel that lies hidden there. It is a path that reaches far beyond and leads to God. Through this channel flows a huge amount of energy, and infinite wisdom.

You do not need to seek power from outside, seek it within you. When God's infinite wisdom is granted to you, what problems, pain, or difficulties will you have? If you are a member of IRH, I recommend as a daily practice that you set aside a time to be quiet, concentrate your thoughts and recite "The Dharma of the Right Mind," our most basic sutra. Then infinite wisdom will well up abundantly from within you. This Dharma has been written in words charged with the energy that comes directly from the life force of Shakyamuni Buddha. It is a manifestation of the wisdom of this great universe. The light of wisdom, the treasure of the human race, reaches you through your golden channel. If such precious Dharma is available to you, aim to be connected to infinite wisdom through this Dharma.

In this way, without seeking power from others or from your external environment, you will be able to carve out a path with your own power. Do not become lost in random thoughts or absorbed in aimless reading; instead, awaken to your own inner wisdom. In order to guide you, I created the "Dharma of the Right Mind." The numerous books I have published are, in a way, aimed at helping you understand this Dharma more deeply. So using those books as a reference to help in your understanding of Truth, I would like you to practice meditating, with the "Dharma of the Right Mind" always beside you. I am sure that you will be granted infinite wisdom and the great light of hope. With bright hope, let us enjoy the breath of spring, in the prime of spring.

6: The Nature of Courage

1. What Is Courage?

In this chapter, I would like to discuss courage. From ancient times, courage has been explained as the strength to cut through difficulties and open up a new way; it has been seen as the driving force to carry through great works. Actually, even if you aspire to do something significant in this world, without courage you will never be able to do so.

Sometimes if you wait patiently, the tide may turn in your favor, but the chances of this happening are slim; this does not generally happen. Rather than taking a passive attitude and simply waiting for your fortune to take a turn for the better, it is much more realistic to make a commitment to take steady steps and to make an effort every day. As you continue to hold this positive attitude, the future will open up for you.

Since you were born into this world with the purpose of your spiritual improvement, why should you not take the initiative and live positively? It is useful once in a while to think about courage, and check to see how courageous you are at present. Courage is a synonym for bravery or inner resolution. A readiness to face difficulties is characteristic of this quality, and this often serves as a golden axe that cuts a way through a path of thorns that lies ahead of you.

In many cases, life's difficulties originate from seeing yourself wrongly, as small or weak, or seeing yourself as someone who can be overwhelmed by problems. Often you make the mistake of identifying with a fragile image of yourself, but this does not reflect your true stature.

Your true self is essentially free of limitation, and your true power is the same as that of God. Human beings are the children of God. We are gifted with the same creative power as God, but most people are blind to this Truth. They mistake themselves for limited beings, underestimate their potential power, and confine their abilities within narrow boundaries. If they face adversity, they often attribute their lack of success to a lack of ability, to circumstances, or to their relationships with others.

If you look at your situation from a higher perspective, you will understand that the real cause of your difficulties is not always to be found in outside factors; often it is a lack of will power. If you are weak-willed, you will have difficulty overcoming adversity. You should look carefully to check whether other people or circumstances are responsible for your unhappiness, or whether your unhappiness is because you did not take the initiative, you did not stand up and open the door.

2 . Compassion and Courage

Next, I would like to discuss problems that may arise in connection with courage and brave actions, for boldness may sometimes harm others. The theme of this discussion will be compassion and courage, or gentleness and courage.

Those who are gentle tend to lack courage. Because of their sensitivity to the feelings of others, they often behave the way that other people expect, and they tend to sympathize with other people's opinions. As a result of trying to please everybody, gentle people risk falling under the influence of those who are stronger, and may eventually lose their identity. However, such a person does not truly understand gentleness. Although gentleness can easily be confused with a lack of resolution, these two qualities are actually quite different.

Let us now re-examine the true meaning of "gentleness" and "compassion." Is it really being gentle to go along with whatever another asks you to do? Of course, if a person goes along with whatever you want, you tend to find that person gentle and likeable. However, it is doubtful whether such an accepting attitude encourages us to grow and improve.

Take university students as an example. At the beginning of each school year, freshmen proudly come to the campus, filled with expectations. The source of their joy is the satisfaction that their hard work has been rewarded and that they have been admitted to a university to study.

Some may argue it is cruel to sift aspiring candidates through a strict screening process, and that anybody who wishes to study at university should be admitted. There have always been people who claim that educational institutions should offer the opportunity to study to everybody who wishes to do so. However, looking realistically at the current state of university education, the limit on the number of admissions is unavoidable, because of constraints on the numbers of teaching staff, the limited facilities, and other such factors.

Is it good or bad to screen students for admission to universities? I think it is important to look at the aims of university education. The main goal is to cultivate the abilities of students, so they can make a meaningful contribution to society. In light of this, I would say it makes sense to choose those candidates who have the higher qualifications and abilities.

Some may still protest that discriminating in this way is merciless and heartless; they need to understand that real joy is born of overcoming difficulties. We can never refine our souls in circumstances that are easy or favorable for us. Today's society is very competitive, but we must not overlook the way in which competition works. It is, as I have said, like a whetstone to polish our souls. If we remain content with lukewarm relationships in which we "lick one another's wounds," our souls will never evolve.

Sometimes, you may need to be stern. For example, if you see something about a person that needs to be corrected, you have to let them know. In a case like this, you have to understand that sometimes a telling-off is an expression of love. It is not love or being kind to accept everything that others ask of you. If you think someone is on the verge of going astray unless you point out how to get back on track, you have to be decisive and give that person a serious talking-to. This is how compassion expresses itself temporarily in the form of courage.

There is a difference between being angry and telling someone off. It is certainly not in harmony with Truth to vent your anger on someone, but you cannot always be smiling and it is sometimes necessary to reprimand others. At work, a boss may sometimes reprimand a subordinate not because he hates him, but rather because it is necessary for the future, to ensure that work will be done properly or that the office will be managed better. In this case, the boss's act, the reprimand, is an expression of compassion.

We should not only aim to cultivate a soft, gentle character; it is necessary to understand that compassion is based on strength and courage. Salvation in the truest sense requires the courage to say what should be said, and the strength to advise another to correct what needs to be corrected. We should not be coldhearted in our relations with others, but we need to understand that when decisive comments and actions are required it is necessary to be emotionally detached.

If you face a difficulty with someone and a candid comment would be sufficient to correct the situation, you may lack the resolution to speak up. The result is increased pain for both parties. This sort of relationship is unhealthy and fruitless. So that both people in a relationship grow, you sometimes have to have the courage and strength to reprimand another, to correct what has been wrongly done.

We need to understand what being compassionate and being brave have in common. Also we need to understand how compassion and courage are two different expressions of the same attitude, instead of seeing them as completely unrelated to one another.

3. Leadership

Now, let us look at the issue of leadership. The meaning of leadership is having the ability to influence and guide people, and show them the path to follow. There have been various expressions of leadership in different eras, but never in history has there been a time when leadership was as keenly needed as it is today.

Leadership is the ability to guide people on God's behalf. It is the will of God that guides, educates, and nurtures people, and His will manifests on Earth through the work of leaders. Accordingly, leaders on Earth should always make a great effort to cultivate their divine nature so they can guide people's development, on God's behalf, and help them to become stronger and more resolute, to open their eyes to the Truth.

What is the secret of leadership? I think the secret lies in a leader's charisma—in other words, in some quality of character that appeals to people. The ability to lead is not determined by birth, intellectual abilities, or appearance, but by a person's spiritual qualities. Actually, your character does its own work, to a much greater extent than you are aware of. When people try to understand you, they do not necessarily judge you after examining your background thoroughly; they feel the energy of your character, and judge what kind of person you are.

Leadership has its basis in the power of a person's character to influence others. Leaders must be sensitive to the atmosphere they create around them, because the ability to lead others does not derive from social status or financial power, but from a profound intelligence and a spiritual refinement that underlie the whole personality.

4. The Ability to Make Decisions

One of the important requirements of a leader is the ability to make decisions. A good leader is always a good decision maker, and there are no exceptions. If you are unable to make decisions and take action when necessary, you risk missing out on a large portion of life's treasure that you may have been able to enjoy. If you take too much time to consider every possibility before reaching a decision, you may miss the chance of a lifetime. If you wish to be a leader, you should be capable of making quick decisions, based on a superior ability to foresee future implications.

Making quick decisions does not simply mean choosing between left and right; it involves the ability to think out the best way to proceed amid ever changing circumstances and the march of time, and, if a decision turns out to be wrong, to correct it. In this context, the ability to make good decisions is a synonym for thoughtfulness, although very often people confuse thoughtfulness with indecision. The ability of a true leader to make decisions requires judgment to solve complicated problems from a broader perspective. A true leader brings that broad perspective to deal with practical day-to-day problems as well. This is based on a careful observation of circumstances, and the constant adjustment of decisions that have already been made.

Actually, the greater a leader, the more ready he or she is to accept that errors do occur in the making of decisions, and to correct them. Being good at decision making does not mean never changing what has already been decided; being a leader who can make good decisions does not mean being stubborn. Although good leaders must have the courage of their convictions, they must also be prepared to examine whether their decisions are really in accordance with God's will and whether they themselves are working for the well-being of other people, or whether their true intentions are to fulfill their own egotistical desires.

The basis of all a true leader's decisions must be love that wishes to nurture people. As a leader, you may sometimes be compelled to make decisions that are not advantageous to you; at times you will have to admit that you made a mistake or have taken wrong action. Because human beings are proud, it is rather hard for us to admit our faults or failures. However, everybody makes inappropriate remarks that hurt others, or makes a slip of the tongue at some time or other. On such occasions, you should not think about how to protect your ego or be attached to your reputation; you should have the courage to change your decision for the sake of the well-being of others. This openness will then generate the power to make the next decision.

I believe there are two keys to living a successful life: firstly a will of iron that allows you to overcome any difficulty, and secondly, a flexibility that enables you to adjust your attitudes in response to quickly changing circumstances. Actually, many of those who have achieved great success have possessed both keys; they have had the flexibility to adapt to changing circumstances, while steadfastly following the path they believed in.

If you lack flexibility of mind and cannot easily adjust to different environments, you will not be highly successful although you may enjoy smaller scale, short-term successes. If you wish to achieve long-term success, remember these two keys.

5. The Importance of Courage

In this final section, let us consider the importance of courage from two angles. Firstly, courage is indispensable in preventing evil from gathering force, because evil feeds on human weakness, on cowardice and indecision. It is undeniable that human beings have a tendency to take advantage of another's weakness. Face to face with somebody over whom we feel we could easily get the upper hand, we are all tempted to a greater or lesser extent to say too much or to demand too much from such a person. If that person gives the impression of being weak, it tends to feed the destructive impulses that exist in everybody, so it is important not to give others the chance to take advantage of us.

Living modestly is fine, but we should not be cowardly or irresolute. We should not be afraid of other people's criticism or concerned only about protecting ourselves, otherwise we will never be able to achieve anything of significance. Nobody who has achieved greatness has been without criticism and accusations from others. However, do you think great figures spent sleepless nights worrying over their reputations? It is unlikely. At times they probably felt hurt, but they continued advancing in their own way and fulfilled their mission.

Here is something important to remember; if you are always prepared to adjust your attitudes to changing circumstances, and keep moving forward with firm steps, people will gradually give up criticizing and accusing you. Then some day, the fierce criticism will subside and turn to admiration. As we probe human psychology, we often find that criticism and accusation are really disguised admiration.

We do not say anything against a person whose success does not have any impact on us. If, on the other hand, someone's success seems to hurt our feelings, or makes us feel inferior or disadvantaged, we tend to feel we want to find fault in that person. So, when you are under fierce attack and being criticized by others, first reflect deeply on yourself. Then, if you think you are not to blame, do not be afraid to advance on the path you believe in. Also, do not forget that criticism is admiration in disguise, and that there are also people who understand and accept you.

The second reason courage is important is that it is indispensable in creating utopia on Earth. This world is a material world, and it is quite difficult to attain spiritual self-realization. Very often people are attached to and misled by the things of this world and go astray; so without courage and a strong will, we will never be able to create utopia. We must be strong in order to continue spreading Truth without being swayed by criticism.

Courage is one of the tools necessary for the construction of utopia on Earth. It works like a chisel or a plane, like an ax or a saw in building the great structure. Remember to look at courage in this way and always check to see if you are trying to build your spiritual edifice with the right tools.

If you ever find yourself complaining that things are not going as well as you would wish, or that you are constantly running into obstacles as you strive to spread the teachings of Truth, check to see whether you have the tool of courage ready, or whether you have forgotten it. Aspiration and a strong will are indispensable for cutting a path through to the future. Without strength of will, it is impossible to lead a constructive and positive life.

BUSINESS REPLY MAIL

FIRST-CLASS MAIL PERMIT NO. 7325   NEW YORK, NY

POSTAGE WILL BE PAID BY ADDRESSEE

Lantern Books
1 Union Square West, Suite 201
New York, NY 10003

✓ Yes! I want to become happy!

Please send me a free booklet by Ryuho Okawa with clues that will help me attain true happiness—NOW!

Name: Mr / Mrs / Ms / Miss _____

Address: _____

City: _____ State: ____ ZIP: ____

7: Living a Positive Life

1. The Frontier Spirit

In this chapter, let us focus on ways to live positively and courageously, and cut through difficulties. First, I would like to explain the term "frontier spirit." This was first used several hundred years ago when the early settlers in North America advanced boldly westward. Even today frontier spirit is still relevant and has a strong attraction for us.

It is important to identify the frontiers in your own life. When you practice self-reflection, you need to recognize how far you have come and in which direction you wish to move. Those who recognize their own frontiers can identify problems and get ready to solve them, while those who do not have a frontier spirit remain stuck, or continue to live monotonously and take everything for granted. Only with a willingness to live positively and accept challenges can you break new ground and start new projects. Those who have a frontier spirit are also the people who can see that this very moment is the frontier from which the future of the whole of humanity will open out.

I would like to ask each of you, the readers of this book: Where is your frontier? Where is the base camp from which you will move forward into a world that has no limits? What plans do you have to step forward into the fertile lands of life that lie ahead of you? What problems stand in your way, and how are you going to solve them? You need to know clearly where your frontiers lie, which area you want to move into, and what stands in your way.

It is very easy for human beings to forget to make an effort and to slip into mediocrity. If you find this tendency in yourself, it is important to summon the frontier spirit. The most miserable life imaginable for a human being would be to repeat the same things monotonously day after day, without ever trying anything new, because of an inability to find any positive meaning in life. Living in this way you do not make any contribution, neither do you win any admiration for tedious repetition, day in, day out.

To those lost in mediocrity, the frontier spirit may sound like something revolutionary, but, without it, no one has ever achieved great things. All the people who were responsible for great achievements—be they politicians, religious leaders or scientists—had that frontier spirit. They never lost sight of the area they wanted to move into, the risks or obstacles they needed to anticipate and how to overcome them. Always be aware of where your "frontier" lies.

2. Invincible Thinking—Winning in Every Situation

I asked you to consider what obstacles might block your way. Now I would like to introduce a new perspective. At times, you may feel that you are under attack or that you are being hurt or criticized by others, but it is important to remember this is not a matter of life and death. It is good to remember what happens in movies; the actors and actresses appear to be dead after a fight, but as soon as the film comes to an end, they begin to talk together in a friendly way. Similarly, anyone who appears to be your enemy or to stand in your way is not really an enemy; that person is only playing a temporary role to teach you a particular lesson.

Take a moment and think how many people in this world actually intend to cause harm or create serious trouble. People sometimes harm others, but they usually do so unintentionally. This applies even to those who commit crimes; all of them have reasons in their defense. No one wants to see themselves as an out-and-out villain.

The truth is that every human being wants to be loved. When this wish to be loved comes into conflict with someone else's wish to be loved, a feeling close to hate may arise, or the two people may become locked in competition. However, this negative emotion does not last long. There is only one truth: everyone, without exception, wants to live happily. Essentially, there is no enemy to hate, nor any wall to block your way.

There were no walls blocking the way of the great scientist Isaac Newton. Albert Einstein once said of Newton that he was a fortunate man because nature was like an open book to him, and he had no trouble reading it. Einstein's remark indicates that truth exists just as it is, ready for people to discover, and that actually, no obstacles stand in the way to finding it.

In this world, there are no tangible obstacles that block your way. You may have an image of yourself being obstructed by someone or something, and you may see other people or your environment as factors that deliberately bar your way. But these things are not real. Essentially, there are no enemies to hate, nor is there anything in your environment that has the intention of upsetting you.

It may help your understanding if you think about your job. When you try and accomplish something you may face difficulties, but solutions are already in store and the chance of your getting into a real crisis is slim. There are millions of companies in the world, and every day and night different dramas unfold in each one of them. Although they constantly face difficulties, not many of them actually go bankrupt. Often, solutions are found through the efforts of the people involved and a new path opens in an unexpected way.

A useful attitude to adopt is that no one in this world has ever failed. Every individual is born into this earthly world with the purpose of refining his or her soul through various experiences, so there can be no such thing as failure. Realize you are playing a temporary role in this world. You are just like an actor or an actress in a movie and nothing can really harm you. All the events that occur in this world serve as lessons for you and provide you with spiritual nourishment. If you can see life from this perspective, you will be able to find your true self, the part of you which never feels discouraged or lost.

I would like to call this way of thinking "Invincible Thinking." With this attitude you can always win. No matter what the circumstances, you can be a winner in every situation if you can learn from every facet of your life. I recommend that you master this way of thinking.

3. A Positive Attitude

In addition to Invincible Thinking, I would like to explain the importance of having a positive attitude. Very often, the circumstances around you reflect your state of mind. Those who always look for bad news or are constantly afraid of failure will find an environment that corresponds to their inner images. This is why children who are susceptible to bullying are bullied wherever they go.

If you have an image of yourself as miserable, other people will almost certainly want to bully you. If, on the other hand, others always praise you, an aura that attracts praise will develop around you, so that even if you move to a new place, you will be praised there, too.

People sense the aura around you. If you want to be one of life's winners in all situations, you must have the air of success. As long as you learn from every situation and try to find the seeds of success in every failure, you will never be a loser.

The inventor and genius Thomas Edison once said that although thousands of his experiments failed before he finally invented the light bulb, they were all lessons, and that each failure showed him a method that was not successful. They were not just simple repetitions of failure, and through them he came to understand how to succeed. Having such a positive attitude gives you great power to live successfully.

Do you think it is good to lead a mediocre life? Do you really think that a life in which nothing happens is wonderful?

Could you really be grateful for a life like that? You may face problems that at the time seem almost impossible to solve, but once the crisis has passed, they become spiritual nourishment. Actually, these experiences are as precious as diamonds. It is important to derive as much spiritual nourishment as possible from every situation, so do not make the mistake of seeing yourself as one of life's losers by seeing your experiences as setbacks or failures.

Some people always pity themselves and want to see themselves as tragic heroes or heroines. They can never find true happiness because their sense of unhappiness is too strong and they always seek sympathy from others. If they make a small mistake at work, they see it as an enormous problem. If they hear someone of the opposite sex make a negative remark about them, they feel rejected, and think that life is not worth living. Then they stray into dark mazes. Many people react like this.

Look once more at the image you have of yourself, and check to see if you have a tendency to self-pity. Self-pity will never bring you happiness; instead, it will lead you into a world of nostalgia and misplaced sympathy.

Do you remember being sick and feverish when you were small? If you do, try to remember the feeling you had at that time. Did you not feel more satisfied when your fever became higher? With a higher fever, it was perhaps easier for you to tell your friends why you were absent from school. Deep down, you may have felt like a tragic hero, and perhaps thought that if you stayed in bed for three days with a very high fever you would win the admiration of all your friends.

This mental tendency may surface in many situations. At critical moments, people who have this tendency may get sick or unconsciously try to find excuses for their failure. For example, they may catch a cold just before an important examination, or become sick before a big match. On the day of a big date, they may show up pale from lack of sleep.

Many people repeat such behavior again and again. Deep down, they think of themselves as losers and always prepare reasons for their failure in advance. They imagine they feel a certain degree of happiness at being consoled by others instead of being praised. Those who always have excuses ready and see themselves as constantly failing will never attain true happiness.

If you have a tendency to self-pity and draw sympathy to you because you are unhappy, you must have the courage to change. You do not need sympathy from others. What you must do is to create an image of yourself as a person who is always happy, constructive, and active.

On a cold winter's day, you can see plum trees covered with snow. Although the blossoms may be hidden, when the snow falls from the branches, the flowers open beautifully. Like them, you should be courageous even when the snows of life fall upon you. You should reveal your true form, the beautiful flowers, by shaking off the snow. Stop complaining about the cold, saying you will freeze to death because snow is falling on you and covering your flowers. Instead just shake your branches to reveal your beautiful blossoms. Only with a positive attitude like this will you be able to create true happiness.

4. The Snowball Effect

While on the subject of snow, I would like to introduce you to my way of looking at the snowball effect. Every day, many things happen, and these events can be the seeds of good fortune and happiness or the seeds of trouble and anxiety. However, if you always try to learn the lesson and find the seeds of success in every situation, no matter what happens, you will grow in the same way as a snowball that expands automatically as it rolls downhill.

Even if pebbles and dirt get mixed in with the snowball, they do not stop it getting bigger and bigger. As it keeps rolling, the snowball increases in size by gathering fresh snow. To compare life to a snowball is very valuable, because it will inspire you to develop great stature. Remember that if you keep on rolling, without worrying about the pebbles and dirt, you will grow.

If someone points out your negative traits, it is no use crying endlessly. Either you should accept the criticism or reject it. You should remain undisturbed and examine the reason for the criticism. Then, if you think that the misunderstanding belongs to the other person, you do not have to accept it. You may need to sort out the misunderstanding and explain it. However, if you think what the other person has said is right, despite the fact that you may not want to accept it, look at yourself once again and trust that you are being taught a valuable lesson.

Some of you may be bothered by your sensitivity to spiritual beings, or troubled by the influence of bad spirits from lower realms. If this is the case, I recommend you change your attitude and become more positive. You can even use a bad spirit as your tutor. A haunting teaches you that you are not yet enlightened. If you are influenced by bad spirits, it means that you are not happy and care-free; you are worried or frustrated. A spirit comes as a tutor to haunt you so that you can see what your problems are. If you clear away the worries in your heart and live positively, the bad spirit will leave.

It is very important to see every situation you face and every person you meet in this life as a teacher. There are also people who show you how not to behave. When you meet someone wonderful, it is necessary to respect him or her and try to learn from their good points. On the other hand, when you meet someone you would not wish to emulate, try to observe the negative aspects of character and check to see that you do not have these same traits. If you find these traits in yourself, resolve to correct them.

If you adopt this attitude, every person you meet in life can be a teacher to you. Every relationship you are in will be a study that benefits you. Of course, everyone wishes they could meet just those people they like, not those they dislike. If, however, you cannot avoid meeting people you dislike, it is a good idea to study their problems and look at what makes them seem to be troublemakers, then try to act in the opposite way. This is important for successful living.

If you meet someone who has had a failure in managing a business, learn why the person failed so that you can take precautions. If you see someone has failed in an environment similar to yours, you can learn how to avoid the same predicament. If you see someone in a different situation who is successful, you can also learn a great deal from them. Life will keep providing more and more opportunities for you to encounter all kinds of people. With this attitude of interest and discovery, victory is inevitable—you will constantly walk toward the light.

5. Time to Take Flight into Infinity

In the final section, I remind you that there are times to take flight into infinity. At times, you need to reflect on yourself and examine whether you are imposing limits on your own abilities, because it is easy to get caught by this negative pattern of thinking. Many people tend to think: "I have never been loved by someone of the opposite sex, so in the future it will not be any different." or "I have never been successful at study or work, so in the future, I will not be successful," or "I was never praised before, so I never will be praised."

To these people, I want to ask why they have such a negative self-image. Why are you attached to this negative self-image? Why do you pay more attention to your negative self-image than to your true self? Is it really so important? Are you living the life you wish to live? Have you imprisoned yourself by intentionally placing limits on yourself?

In your life, there are moments to take flight into infinity. Above all, it is important to take full command of your thoughts. If you can turn your thoughts to the light and start living positively, you will be able to solve all your problems. Also, do not underestimate the importance of cooperation with others.

In China, people often say that fortune is smiling on you when you meet a person who is "precious" to you and brings you good luck. This happens to everybody in this world. You have probably met people who are "precious" in your life and who bring you many opportunities. If thousands of people cooperate in this way, we can achieve many great things. The light of heaven will certainly help those who make the effort to open up their own path. A person who is precious to you can be either someone living on this Earth, or a guardian or guiding spirit. No matter whether they live on this Earth or in the other world, people want to help those who take responsibility for their life, and who live every day actively and enthusiastically.

A company president will have a similar outlook. If he sees one of his employees working hard every day, he will want to promote that person and give them a more responsible job. If, however, he sees someone who wants to be promoted without making any particular effort, the president will have a negative impression and hesitate to promote them. Similarly, if you lead an extremely positive life, you will attract many people to you who will want to help you. Then you will be able to achieve far more than you could ever have achieved on your own.

I would like you to know that there are no limits as to how high you can fly in this life. If you want to fly, you should make a great effort, then help will come to you from others, but before everything comes a positive attitude to life. I have no doubt that this is the key for you to become one of life's winners.

8: The Will of the Great Universe

1. The Galaxy and Human Beings

Finally, let us discuss what we might call "the will of the great universe," and the connection between the universe and we humans who live on planet Earth.

Have you ever looked up at the night sky and cast your thoughts toward the stars that shine there? Perhaps when you were a child, or as a young man or woman, you gazed up at the sky through a window and imagined all kinds of wonderful things. Way out in space is the Milky Way. Perhaps you have experienced a sense of mystery just looking at it. Probably many of you have looked up at the starry sky and experienced a sense of the unfathomable nature of the universe. I myself have long been interested in the heavens, and the sense of mystery that it embodies.

However, we should not remain absorbed in fantasy but look at reality and regard it with new eyes. In looking at reality, I would like to think about time and space. I am not a physicist and so I am not in a position to discuss this subject as a scientist but, still, I have a sense of the unfathomable in relation to time and space.

Let us try to imagine that an inhabitant of a planet far away is gazing at us through a highly advanced telescope. How would our world look through his eyes? If the distance between his planet and our Earth were ten light-years, that would mean he was actually watching us ten years ago. Other beings living on planets that are yet further away would be seeing earthlings of a hundred years ago, two hundred years ago, even several thousand years ago.

On the other hand, when we look through a telescope at the stars, some of them, though they seem to be emitting a bright light now, may not exist any more. The light that they gave out in the past, perhaps hundreds, thousands, or tens of thousands of years ago, may have traveled all that distance and only now be reaching our eyes. Those stars may already be extinct.

Considering such things, we cannot help but think about how vast the universe is and how small we are who live in it. It is an extremely mysterious feeling, but it is an undeniable fact that we are all tiny beings, existing individually in such a vast expanse of universe. It is also true that a small universe exists inside our physical body. It can be said that our heart corresponds to the galaxy to which our planet Earth belongs, and other parts of our body to other groups of stars and planets. From the perspective of a microorganism or a cell, our physical body would look like a vast universe.

Between these two perspectives, the vast and the minute, we are unable to see ourselves objectively. We cannot know for certain whether we are enormous or tiny. It is impossible to measure human existence with an absolute scale. From a greater perspective, the Earth may be as tiny as a cell in a universe, and human beings may be even tinier, like microorganisms living on the cell. I would like you to understand that our lives are so transient and uncertain when we measure them in comparative terms.

2. The Truth about the Three-Dimensional World on Earth

We do live in our galaxy, but it is not enough to consider our existence as human beings in this world only in relation to the Earth and the great universe. In fact, from the perspective of the spirit world ranging from the fourth dimension and higher, our three-dimensional universe looks as if it is no more than an aquarium.

Viewed from the Real World, which embraces this entire universe, our three-dimensional space is like an aquarium placed in a room—the pebbles at the bottom of it may be likened to a group of stars and planets, and one tiny cell of the rock would represent the Sun or the Earth. If viewed on a slightly enlarged scale, human beings would be at most the small fish swimming in the water. I would like to tell you that although we think this universe is so vast, from the perspective of the multi-dimensional world that is formed of the fourth dimension and higher, it is only a small, enclosed world.

You also need to be aware that from the viewpoint of the inhabitants of the Real World, the human beings who dwell in the world of the third dimension look very different. This is because they have a different sense of time. For instance, let us imagine that a certain high spirit comes closer to our world on Earth, with the intention of guiding us. When high spirits watch us, they perceive quite clearly not only our present existence but our past and our future as well, if not completely, then at least to some extent. So, when high spirits look at us, we who live in this world on Earth, our past and future states can be seen overlapping our present existence. It is important to understand that our world looks quite mysterious and uncertain from the perspective of the other world.

When we live completely absorbed in this material world, we tend to take for granted the laws and rules that govern this world and think of them as absolutely fixed. However, the laws that govern every single thing that exists in this world are not necessarily the absolute truth. For instance, the things that we can certainly confirm exist—such as a desk, a chair, a building, the ground, or a mountain—can look quite different if viewed from the perspective of higher dimensions. Overlapping their present existence, future states may be revealed, for instance, when they will be destroyed and disappear, or past states, such as before they came into existence.

When a spirit who belongs to a higher dimension looks at the desk in front of you, it may see the desk being destroyed in the future, or being built into a desk, or even the tree growing on a mountain that the desk is made of. There are actually spirits who specialize in determining the original state of materials that constitute the things of this world.

I would like you to know that the past, present, and the future can exist in the same space, and that such an unusual perspective can exist. We do indeed exist in an uncertain world, uncertain both in terms of size and the passage of time. I would like you to be aware that in this uncertain world, we only swim or just flow in the stream of time.

3. Get Rid of Vanity

If the time and space we inhabit are so uncertain, which ideas are most important for us to remember? What do we need to keep in mind, we who live on planet Earth that is as tiny as a poppy seed, compared to the entire universe, which, in turn, is completely enclosed inside a vast multi-dimensional world?

I would like to summarize the idea that is most important for us in one phrase—"get rid of vanity." By vanity I mean the trivial values connected with our earthly way of life. When we shed the vanity that originates from values and ways of thinking that are valid only in this three-dimensional world, we will start to see our true being. Now, let us look at our lives and consider what it means to be vain.

The greatest vanity of all must be our sense of values, or typically, the sense of our own importance. There are many means of measuring this importance, such as social status, academic records and income. We should know that there are two distinct sets of standards for measuring values—the values connected to Truth and values connected to usefulness in this earthly world. That which embraces both sets of values is also valued in the other world. On the other hand, that which is valuable only in terms of practical utility in this world will often be deemed vain, from the perspective of the other world.

Some of those who have attained high social status are also respected in light of the values of the other world. It is true that some of the leaders of this world will continue to lead others when they return to the other world. So, the fact that a person is a president of a company or a high government official does not necessarily mean that he is living a life of vanity.

However, it is also true that others who have a high social status may be concerned solely with selfish desires for worldly power or recognition. The social status of this type of person is only of worldly value; it does not embrace the values of Truth or the values of the other world.

When we look at things of this world, it is important for us to examine whether they possess values that are appreciated only in this world, or whether they encompass values of Truth that are appreciated in the other world, too. Money must also be examined in the same way. If we are interested only in quantities of money, it simply translates into practical utility in this world. However, when money is spent to realize a high ideal, then values of Truth are created.

In this way, we can shed new light on our sense of values. To do this, we need to get rid of any bias that influences our way of thinking. Traditionally, Buddhism calls this practice "self-reflection"—reflecting upon oneself and striving to eliminate any vanity. If you find yourself attached to something in particular, then it is necessary to examine whether your attachment is entirely vanity or whether there is some value in it. It is necessary to compare the positive and the negative implications and examine whether your attempt to benefit yourself may cause harm to others. There is no end to the subjects you should reflect on.

Self-reflection is indispensable as a practice for each and every one of us to get rid of vanity. If we do not do this while we are living in this world, then when we return to the other world we will be forced to face any vanity in our being. So, I would like you to consider each day as the smallest separate unit of your life and, at the end of every day, humbly examine whether you have been conceited or concerned with vanity.

4. Starting with Nothing, Empty-Handed

In thinking about vanity, a thought comes into my mind every so often. It seems that human beings tend to be ungrateful and take so many things for granted. When we think about the future, we treat our past experiences, the things and money we have already acquired, as preconditions for this.

People who earn thirty thousand dollars a year are usually concerned about how they could earn more, but they never think about a situation where they have no income at all. Others who own businesses tend to take their present turnover for granted. They may think about what they are going to do from now on, but they usually take for granted the fundamental fact that the business exists at all.

As I come into contact with people who suffer from worries and troubles, I recognize that their problems stem from their attitude of taking their current situation for granted, without appreciating it at all. You may meet someone who complains about their husband or wife, but they will usually take their current circumstances—for example their financial standing, the house to live in, or their children—for granted. Then they will criticize their partner for a lack of caring.

Have they ever done the mental exercise of looking again at their current situation with fresh eyes, imagining themselves without what they now have, imagining what would have become of them if they had never met their partners, had a house, or if their children had never been born? Perhaps they were able to marry without any problems because their parents were healthy. What would have happened if their parents had died shortly after they were born? As they go through these mental exercises, they will become aware that the circumstances that they consider a source of suffering are something they must not take for granted.

In this way, from the perspective of a third person, to the eyes of God or an inhabitant of a higher spiritual realm, our suffering often seems unjustified. Our state can be likened to that of a person whose hands are full but who still tries desperately to carry more baggage. Although the person is carrying baggage in his right hand and in his left, and also carrying a heavy load on his back, as he comes on a pile of treasure he tries desperately to pick it up and carry it back home. That is how we often appear from a spiritual perspective.

When we are faced with suffering, it is extremely important to get rid of any vanity and go back to the starting point, where we started out with nothing. Try mentally to eliminate everything you take for granted. Try to imagine starting from nothing, with your hands empty. Stand empty-handed. After you have thrown away the baggage you have been holding, what will be left? Your academic record is one example of such baggage. If you graduated from a prestigious university, this becomes a precondition for your progress in life. However, if the label "graduate of a prestigious university" were removed, how would you be accepted in society? You would probably not be satisfied.

It is important that we have trust in ourselves but, at the same time, we have to examine whether the factors on which we base our trust can be taken for granted, and what would happen if these preconditions were eliminated. I have experienced this myself. When I left a large Japanese trading firm to start IRH on my own in 1986, I was left "standing empty-handed." At that time, I realized keenly how much benefit I had enjoyed while working as a member of a big corporation. As I thought about what was left after getting rid of all these benefits—my academic studies and achievements as a student, my work experience, the assistance of my colleagues and supervisors, my annual income, and the reputation of my company, and so on—I could not help realizing I had to throw away any vanity and stand alone, empty-handed.

The only foothold I had was my own mind and soul. I could only rely on myself, my own thoughts and actions, nothing else. I started IRH from nothing; now it is about to grow into a worldwide organization. In the midst of this development, I sometimes remember the idea of "standing empty-handed." Starting out with few funds and no one to work for me, this organization has developed to its present scale. Only if we are prepared to go back to the starting point and stand empty-handed once more, no matter what kind of difficulty befalls us, will we never suffer. I often encourage myself with these thoughts.

5. The Will of the Great Universe

I have considered human beings from both macro- and micro-perspectives, and here I would like to reveal an important truth to you. From the perspective of the great universe, we might seem as tiny bacteria, living on a minute planet that is only a cell in the universe, but nevertheless the "will of the great universe" flows through each and every one of us. It is very important to understand this.

Quantitative measurement, whether big or small, has nothing to do with judging the importance of something. It is more crucial to know what underlies it, or what the core concept is. As long as your core beliefs are right, you will surely be able to walk the path to success.

We are tiny beings compared to this great universe or the vast spirit world. However, as long as the very core of our character, which governs our thoughts and actions, is truthful, this means our thoughts and deeds will be connected to the will of the great universe, and make some contribution to it.

We can be both vast and minute beings. But setting aside these perspectives, we always need to reflect on ourselves and see whether the central core of our being is manifesting the light, the flame of Truth. As long as the core that exists within us is connected to the will of the great universe, finds its origin in the great will and manifests it, there is nothing to be afraid of.

If you continue to live in this world on Earth courageously and steadfastly, but with a readiness to go back to the starting point and stand empty-handed whenever necessary, then a way will open before you and lead you to the great path of success. The question is whether the central core within you is in tune with the will of the great universe that is continually manifesting the powers of creation, nurture, development, and prosperity in our lives.

Make a constant effort to harmonize your will with the will of the great universe, and in this way you can continue to walk on the path to happiness.

WHAT IS IRH?

The Institute for Research in Human Happiness (IRH) is an organization of people who aim to cultivate their souls and deepen their wisdom. The teachings of IRH are based on the spirit of Buddhism. The two main pillars are the attainment of spiritual wisdom and the practice of "love that gives."

Keep updated with
IRH MONTHLY
featuring a lecture by Ryuho Okawa. Each volume also includes a question-and-answer session with Ryuho Okawa on real life problems.

For more information, please contact local offices of IRH.

Also available
MEDITATION RETREATS
Educational opportunities are provided to people who wish to seek the path of Truth. The Institute organizes meditation retreats for English speakers in Japan and other countries.

THE INSTITUTE FOR RESEARCH IN HUMAN HAPPINESS

Kofuku-no-Kagaku

Tokyo
1-2-38 Higashi Gotanda
Shinagawa-ku
Tokyo 141-0022
Japan
Tel: 81-3-5793-1729
Fax: 81-3-5793-1739
Email: JDA02377@nifty.com
www.irhpress.co.jp

New York
2nd Fl. Oak Tree Center
2024 Center Avenue
Fort Lee, NJ 07024
U.S.A.
Tel: 1-201-461-7715
Fax: 1-201-461-7278

Los Angeles
Suite 104
3848 Carson Street
Torrance, CA 90503
U.S.A.
Tel: 1-310-543-9887
Fax: 1-310-543-9447

San Francisco
San Francisco Temple
525 Clinton St.
Redwood City, CA 94062
Tel/Fax: (650) 363-2777
E-mail: sf@irh-intl.org
HP: http://www.irh-sf.org

Hawaii
419 South St. #101
Honolulu, HI 96813
U.S.A.
Tel: 1-808-587-7731
Fax: 1-808-587-7730

Toronto
484 Ravineview Way
Oakville, Ontario L6H 6S8
Canada
Tel / Fax: 1-905-257-3677

London
65 Wentworth Avenue
Finchley, London N3 1YN
United Kingdom
Tel : 44-20-8346-4753
Fax: 44-20-8343-4933

Sao Paulo
(Ciencia da Felicidade do
Brasil)
Rua Gandavo
363 Vila Mariana
Sao Paulo, CEP 04023-001
Brazil
Tel: 55-11-5574-0054
Fax: 55-11-5574-8164

Seoul
178-6 Songbuk-Dong
Songbuk-ku, Seoul
Korea
Tel: 82-2-762-1384
Fax: 82-2-762-4438

Melbourne
P.O.Box 429 Elsternwick
VIC 3185
Australia
Tel / Fax: 61-3-9503-0170

ABOUT THE AUTHOR

Ryuho Okawa, founder and spiritual leader of the Institute for Research in Human Happiness (IRH), has devoted his life to the exploration of the spirit world and ways to human happiness.

He was born in 1956 in Tokushima, Japan. After graduating from Tokyo University, he joined a major Tokyo based trading house and studied international finance at City University of New York. In 1986, he renounced his business career and established IRH.

He has been designing IRH spiritual workshops for people from all walks of life, from teenagers to business executives. He is known for his wisdom, compassion and commitment to educating people to think and act in spiritual and religious ways.

The members of IRH follow the path he teaches, ministering to people who need help by spreading his teachings.

He is the author of many books and periodicals, including *The Laws of the Sun*, *The Golden Laws*, and *The Laws of Eternity*. He has also produced successful feature length films (including animations) based on his works.